# BROWN v. BOARD OF EDUCATION

# Brown v. Board of Education

## THE BATTLE FOR INTEGRATION

by
Mark V. Tushnet

Historic Supreme Court Cases
FRANKLIN WATTS
A Division of Grolier Publishing
New York London Hong Kong Sydney
Danbury, Connecticut

*Frontispiece*: NAACP lawyers (left to right) E. C. Hayes, Thurgood Marshall, and James A. Nabrit, Jr., on the steps of the Supreme Court following the ruling in the *Brown v. Board* case that school segregation is unconstitutional.

Photographs copyright ©: New York Public Library, Schomburg Collection: frontis; UPI/Bettmann: pp. 10, 31, 42, 46, 50, 55, 59, 63, 69 top, 76, 81, 98, 100; Library of Congress: p. 22; NAACP: p. 28; The Collection of the Supreme Court of the United States: pp. 69 bottom, 79, 93 (all Harris and Ewing), 121 (Simmie L. Knox); Dwight D. Eisenhower Library/National Park Service: p. 89; The Bettmann Archive: p. 104: Arkansas History Commission: p. 118.

Library of Congress Cataloging-in-Publication Data

Tushnet, Mark V., 1945–
    Brown v. Board of Education: the battle for integration / by Mark V. Tushnet
        p.   cm.—(Historic Supreme Court Cases)
    Includes bibliographical references and index.
    Summary: Describes the people playing major roles in the battle for desegregation, the smaller court cases that led up to Brown v. The Board of Education, and the results and repercussions of the case.
        ISBN 0-531-11230-6
        1. Brown, Oliver, 1918–   —Trials, litigation, etc.—Juvenile literature. 2. Topeka (Kan.). Board of Education—Trials, litigation, etc.— Juvenile literature. 3. Segregation in education—Law and legislation —United States—Juvenile literature. [1. Segregation in education— Law and legislation. 2. Afro-Americans—Civil rights.] I. Title. II. Series.
KF228.B76T87  1995
344.73'0798'0269—dc20
[347.3047980269]                                              95-13013  CIP  AC

# CONTENTS

# Chapter 1
# A LITIGATION CAMPAIGN BEGINS

Barbara Johns was angry. Sixteen years old in 1951, she had been attending high school in Farmville, Virginia, and in the spring she got fed up with her school's facilities. Because enrollments had recently increased, the Prince Edward County school board, which ran the high school, had made some students go to classes in wood and tarpaper shacks on the school grounds. Students had to read used books, and didn't have much equipment for science classes. The school's buses broke down all the time, and students never knew when they would get to school. The board promised to build a new school, but it had not gotten around to it yet.

Barbara decided that somehow she had to put pressure on the school board. She talked with other students and decided to organize a strike: Students would not attend classes until the board built a new high school. She and her friends in the student council kept their plans secret until April 23, 1951. That morning the principal got a phone call telling him that two high school students would get in trouble if the principal did not come to their rescue downtown. He left school to see what had happened.

Barbara immediately got the strike going. She and her friends sent notes to each classroom telling the teachers that there would be a school assembly at eleven in the auditorium. The teachers saw the notes, with what looked like the principal's signature, and went with their classes to the assembly. When they got there, Johns and her friends asked them to leave. Most of the teachers did, and the ones who wouldn't go on their own were escorted out of the room.

Barbara started her talk by denouncing the school board. The students, she said, deserved a real high school, not a school with shacks in the yard. They should boycott the school until the school board did something about it.

Later that day someone called Oliver Hill, a prominent lawyer from Richmond, Virginia, who happened to be nearby, getting ready to file a case in a neighboring county. Hill's caller asked him for legal advice: Would the students be put in jail for violating the state's compulsory education laws? Could they somehow get the school board to upgrade the school's condition?

Hill was reluctant to take the case. He certainly didn't want to take on the students as his clients without seeing what their parents wanted. Hill and his partner Spottswood Robinson decided to meet the students. They asked a local preacher, Leslie Francis Griffin, to set up a meeting. When Hill and Robinson got to the meeting at Griffin's church, they discovered that they should not have been concerned about the parents: The church was packed with students and their parents, all enthusiastic about getting some legal help to pressure the school board.

Johns, Griffin, Hill, and Robinson were all African-Americans, and Johns's high school was segregated: The African-American children in Prince Edward County went to Johns's school, while white children attended a school with decent facilities. Segregation laws throughout the South required African-Americans and whites to attend separate schools. They were part of a comprehensive system of "Jim Crow" laws requiring separation on buses and trains, in courthouses, and in restaurants and hotels.

In 1951 African-American students and parents all over the country were as fed up as Barbara Johns. In Topeka, Kansas, in Washington, D.C., in Summerton, South Carolina, and near Wilmington, Delaware, groups of students and parents were getting together to see what they could do about the terrible conditions in their segregated schools. They all began by trying simply to get their school boards to spend more money on the African-American schools—to get them decent equipment, or bus service that actually got the children to school—but they quickly realized that the problem ran deeper. It wasn't that school boards weren't putting enough money into the segregated schools; instead, they decided, the problem was that the schools were segregated. Until segregation ended, they concluded, the schools African-American children attended would never be as good as the ones white children went to.

How, though, could they change the system of segregated schools? Segregation was required by local law. In theory, African-Americans could have

9

Spottswood Robinson (center) and Oliver W. Hill (right),
NAACP lawyers for Barbara Johns, discuss a case.

gotten legislatures to change the laws. But, for decades, African-Americans in the South had been kept from voting, either by laws that made it hard for them to register to vote, or—when legal tactics failed—by sheer terror (several leaders of efforts to register African-Americans had been murdered in the 1940s and early 1950s). So, local lawmakers weren't worried about being thrown out of office if they kept segregation in place.

Also in theory, Congress could have directed states to get rid of segregation. African-Americans *had* been gaining political power in the urban North. During and after World War II, African-Americans moved north to work in war-related industries and in the expanding manufacturing sector. They became an important part of the political coalition supporting President Harry S. Truman, who ran on a strong civil rights platform in 1948 and who had ordered that the armed forces end its own segregated system.

Unfortunately, though, African-American political power in Congress didn't match its influence over the executive branch. Congress was organized around a seniority system. Key posts were held by senators and representatives who had served the longest. These members of Congress could keep proposals they didn't like from ever getting a vote by the full House or Senate. The Democratic party had dominated Southern politics since the turn of the century, when state legislatures adopted laws that kept nearly all African-Americans from voting. White voters remembered the period after the Civil War, when, as they saw it, the Republican party had governed them by force. Consequently whoever got the Democratic nomination was elected, and then faced little opposition in the general elections. As a result, Southern senators and representatives

kept their seats for such a long time that they dominated the legislative process. Getting civil rights
laws through Congress, over the objection of the
Southerners who controlled the key committees,
was simply impossible.

That left the courts.

Under our constitutional system, governments—
local, state, and national—have the *power* to do
lots of things, and operating public schools is one of
the central jobs of state and local governments, but
their power is *limited* by specific constitutional provisions. The First Amendment, for example, says
that governments "shall make no law . . . abridging
the freedom of speech." Sometimes it's easy to tell
when a government has violated the limits the
Constitution creates. No one would have trouble
deciding, for example, that it was unconstitutional
for a school board to adopt a policy of providing a
free public education only to children whose parents swear to support the board's members in their
reelection campaigns. That's an obvious violation of
the First Amendment.

Most constitutional problems aren't that clear,
however. Sometimes that's because the Constitution uses general terms. Barbara Johns's lawyers
had to argue that school segregation violated a
clause in the Constitution barring states from
denying people the "equal protection of the laws."
But what does "equal protection of the laws" really
mean?

In the United States constitutional system, we
ask the courts to tell us what the Constitution
means; that is, to interpret it and apply it to particular problems. This power, known as *judicial
review*, is sometimes controversial. The reason is
clear. Courts step in only after a legislature has

passed a law that somebody challenges on constitutional grounds. The legislature could pass the statute only if a majority of people supported it (unless lots of people were kept from voting, which was the situation in the South when segregation laws were enacted). If a court interprets the Constitution to mean that the law is unconstitutional because it violates someone's constitutional rights, it is keeping a majority of the people from getting what they want.

Despite this, the people of the United States have come to live with the system of judicial review. Partly that's because everyone is afraid that a majority might someday violate one of his or her rights, and people trade restrictions from the courts in exchange for protection of their own rights. Partly it's because we don't have any other good way of policing the limits the Constitution puts on governments. Executive branch officials, such as governors and the president, enforce the laws legislatures pass, but they usually don't decide on their own whether those laws are constitutional.

Judicial review has one special feature that both makes it attractive and causes problems. Federal judges, including the justices of the Supreme Court, have life tenure, which means that voters have no way to kick them out if the judges start misinterpreting the Constitution. The advantage of life tenure is judges won't be influenced much by the political majorities that enact the laws that might violate constitutional rights. Barbara Johns couldn't expect Virginia's legislature to get rid of the segregation laws, because the legislators had to try to get reelected by constituencies with white majorities. When she took her case into federal court, the judges who would decide it didn't have to worry about losing their jobs if they did something a majority didn't like.

The disadvantage of life tenure is the mirror image of its advantage: It presents the risk of "judicial activism." Federal judges don't have to worry about political pressures, true, but what keeps them from simply doing what they want? That is, why won't judges merely act as substitute legislators who don't have to face reelection? The concern is that, although the judges pretend they are interpreting the Constitution, actually all they are doing is forcing the society to accept the policy choices the judges like.

We have some ways to limit this problem, but it can't be eliminated entirely. The president nominates federal judges, and the Senate has to approve their appointment. That means that over the long run, judges won't get too far out of line with what a national political majority wants. (That was important to Barbara Johns's case. She and her lawyers may have believed that a *national* majority probably disagreed with the *local* Southern policies of segregation. In light of national politics in the 1950s, they may have been right.)

We also try to limit judges by insisting that they explain what they do as an interpretation of the Constitution. If they say that school segregation violates the equal protection clause, they have to say *why*. Their explanations have to be tied to the Constitution's text, the intent of the people who adopted it, prior judicial decisions, and perhaps some overall "theory" of what the Constitution is for.

As Barbara Johns's case developed, it tested the limits of judicial review.

After the North won the Civil War, the victors amended the Constitution. Slavery, they knew, was the war's root cause, so they had to get rid of slavery and all its effects. Immediately after the war, the Thirteenth Amendment abolished slavery. That, however, turned out to be insufficient. White governments were reestablished in the South, with the aid of President Andrew Johnson, who had taken office after Abraham Lincoln's assassination. These governments did their best to keep the newly freed slaves in their place, by adopting what were called "Black Codes" that denied African-Americans basic rights such as the right to testify in court. Life for African-Americans under the Black Codes wasn't that different from the way life had been under slavery.

Congress, dominated by Republicans who opposed the president, decided that it had to do something. It adopted a program called Reconstruction, to replace the white-dominated state governments with ones that would respect the rights of African-Americans.

More important in the long run, though, was the Fourteenth Amendment to the Constitution, adopted in 1868. Its first sentence was a simple declaration that everyone born in the United States was a citizen. That stated a principle of equality that the Amendment's next sentence made more specific. That sentence has three clauses. The first says that states can't "abridge the privileges and immunities of citizens of the United States." The next says that they can't deprive anyone of "life, liberty, or property, without due process of law." The final clause says that they can't deny anyone "the equal protection of the laws."

For the Fourteenth Amendment's framers, the "privileges and immunities" clause was probably the most important. They thought that it guaranteed everyone in the country some basic human rights. Exactly what those rights were, though, was unclear. Eight years after the Fourteenth Amendment became part of the Constitution, the Supreme Court gave the "privileges and immunities" clause a narrow interpretation, and it hasn't played much of a part in our law since then.

Instead, people began to focus on the "equal protection" clause, which after all did refer explicitly to equality. What sort of equality did the Constitution guarantee?

The problem is that nearly every law is "unequal" in some sense. A law requiring people under the age of sixteen to attend school treats those people differently from people over sixteen, for example. The question really is not whether the Constitution requires complete equality, but what kinds of inequality it permits. What might justify unequal treatment?

To figure that out, we can think about the *kinds of rights* involved, and the *classifications* of people who are treated unequally. A compulsory attendance law classifies people on the basis of age, and it affects their right to do what they want (go to school, work, or whatever).

The Fourteenth Amendment's framers focused on the kinds of rights. As they thought about the problems African-Americans faced under the Black Codes, the framers decided that all the problems arose because African-Americans were denied *fundamental civil rights*. If African-Americans had full civil and political rights, the framers believed, the problems would disappear.

"Civil rights" meant something different to them than it means to us, though. The amendment's framers thought that there were three kinds of rights: civil rights, political rights, and social rights. Civil rights included the right to own property, to make contracts, and to testify in court.

Political rights included the right to vote, of course, and the right to serve on juries. Social rights were everything else: the right of an employer to hire whomever he or she wanted, the right of a hotel or restaurant to serve whatever clients they chose, and the like.

As Reconstruction-era lawyers understood what they had done in amending the Constitution, the Fourteenth Amendment guaranteed everyone civil rights, but nothing more. It took another constitutional amendment, the Fifteenth (1870), to guarantee that the right to vote would not be denied on account of race.

In our constitutional system, the Supreme Court is the final word on interpreting the Constitution and its amendments. Deciding what rights the Fourteenth Amendment protected would ultimately be the Court's task.

In 1879 the Court began to flesh out what the Fourteenth Amendment meant. West Virginia had a statute that prohibited African-Americans from serving on juries. An African-American challenged his conviction for murder, arguing that the statute deprived him of his Fourteenth Amendment rights. The Supreme Court agreed (*Strauder v. West Virginia,* 1879). Its opinion emphasized the amendment's background, "securing to a race recently emancipated . . . all the civil rights that the superior race enjoy." The amendment "declar[ed] that the law in the States shall be the same for the black as for the white, . . . that no discrimination shall be made against them because of their color." According to the Court, the Fourteenth Amendment was intended to ensure that African-Americans were "exempt[ed] from legal discrimination, implying inferiority in civil society, . . . and [from] discriminations which are steps toward

reducing them to the condition of a subject race."
Laws that treated African-Americans as deserving
less legal protection than whites were unconstitutional.
This decision held that the Fourteenth
Amendment barred states from using a racial *classification* to deny a *political* right. But what about
social rights?

By the time the Supreme Court reached that
question, political circumstances had changed. In
1876, Reconstruction ended. The 1876 election was
extremely close, and there were charges of fraud.
To secure the election of Rutherford B. Hayes,
Republican political leaders made a deal with
Southern Democrats: Hayes would withdraw federal troops from the South and allow Southerners to
take over their governments. Everyone expected
that this would lead to the restoration of white-dominated governments and the exclusion of
African-Americans from political power in the
South, and it did.

Over the next decades the South established
the Jim Crow system that persisted until the middle of the next century. White people north and
south had engaged in widespread private discrimination against African-Americans: They hired
African-Americans only for menial jobs, and
refused to sell houses to African-Americans on the
same terms they offered to whites. The Jim Crow
system wrote this sort of discrimination into law.

One group of Jim Crow laws was designed to
eliminate African-American voting power. Laws
requiring that voters demonstrate their ability to
read and write were put in place for the first time.
Other laws required people to pay an annual poll
tax if they wanted to vote. The most discriminatory
voting restriction was the "grandfather clause":

Southern states required voters to demonstrate their literacy, but then suspended the requirement for anyone whose ancestors had been able to vote before the Civil War; all whites could vote automatically, while African-Americans had to pass a literacy test.

Another group of Jim Crow laws *required* discrimination and segregation. The most important involved segregation in trains and streetcars. These Jim Crow laws required that African-Americans ride on separate train cars, or to take seats in the back of the new electric street railways in Southern cities. Finally, Southern legislatures barred African-American children from attending the same public schools as white children. (The Kentucky legislature eventually went all the way and barred even private colleges from offering an integrated education. In 1908 the Supreme Court rejected a constitutional challenge to this law [*Berea College v. Kentucky*, 1908].)

The Supreme Court had already said, though, that the Fourteenth Amendment was aimed at eliminating laws that subordinated African-Americans. How could these Jim Crow laws be constitutional? After all, they certainly were designed to "reduc[e] them to the condition of a subject race."

In 1896 the Supreme Court upheld the Jim Crow system. In 1890 the Louisiana legislature adopted a statute requiring railroad companies to provide "equal but separate accommodations for the white and colored races" (although it allowed African-American nurses attending white children to ride in the white cars). Homer Plessy, who claimed to be seven-eighths white, decided to test the law's constitutionality by submitting to arrest when he refused to leave the car reserved for whites.

The Supreme Court's decision relied on the Reconstruction-era distinction between civil rights and social rights (*Plessy v. Ferguson*, 1896). According to Justice Henry Brown, the Fourteenth Amendment guaranteed "absolute equality of the two races before the law, but, in the nature of things, it could not have been intended to abolish distinctions based upon color, or to enforce social, as distinguished from political equality." Where a social right like the right to associate in train cars was involved, legislatures could require the separation of the races, Brown wrote, because those laws "do not necessarily imply the inferiority of either race to the other." Indeed, Justice Brown wrote, "if the civil and political rights of both races be equal, one cannot be inferior to the other civilly or politically."

Albion Tourgee, Plessy's lawyer, had urged that segregation laws did indeed embody the white majority's view that African-Americans were inferior. (Tourgee was also a popular writer whose novels dealt with life after the Civil War.) Justice Brown rejected the argument. Its "underlying fallacy," according to Justice Brown, was its "assumption that the enforced separation of the two races stamps the colored race with a badge of inferiority. If this be so, it is not by reason of anything found in the act, but solely because the colored race chooses to put that construction upon it."

Justice Brown's argument may sound ridiculous today, but it made sense to the nation's majority in 1896. Justice Brown also said that Plessy's argument "assumes that social prejudices may be overcome by legislation, and that equal rights cannot be secured to the negro except by an enforced commingling of the two races." Today this seems to overlook the obvious fact that no one was trying to *force* the railroad to "commingle" the races; the only "force" around was exercised by the Louisiana legislature, which was forcing the railroad to separate people it was perfectly willing to allow to commingle. But, again, in 1896 that wasn't how things looked. As Justice Brown put it, the races had "natural affinities," which the legislature was simply following in requiring segregation. "If the two races are to meet upon terms of social equality," Justice Brown wrote, "it must be the result of . . . a mutual appreciation of each other's merits."

Justice John Marshall Harlan, who as a Kentucky aristocrat before the Civil War had owned slaves, wrote one of the most famous dissents in Supreme Court history. "Every one knows," Justice Harlan wrote, "that the statute in question had its origin in the purpose . . . to exclude colored people from coaches occupied by . . . white persons." He was comfortable with the notion that "the white race" was "the dominant race in this country." But, he continued, "in the eye of the law, there is in this country no superior, dominant, ruling class of citizens. There is no caste here. Our constitution is color-blind, and neither knows nor tolerates classes among citizens."

Although *Plessy v. Ferguson* did not involve segregated schools, everyone understood that the Supreme Court had approved the Jim Crow system that included segregated schools. Indeed, at one point Justice Brown had used segregated schools to emphasize his point. To show that segregation did not necessarily imply inferiority, Justice Brown referred to cases upholding segregated schools "even by courts of states where the political rights of the colored race have been longest and most earnestly enforced." Here he cited *Roberts v. Boston,* an 1850 case in which Massachusetts's

Supreme Court justice John Marshall Harlan,
author of the dissent to the *Plessy v. Ferguson*
Supreme Court ruling in 1896

highest court upheld segregated schools. (Justice Brown, himself from Massachusetts, didn't point out that in 1855 the Massachusetts legislature had *banned* segregated schools, in part because it disagreed with the *Roberts* decision.)

*Plessy v. Ferguson* created the "separate but equal" doctrine: Segregated facilities were constitutional—that was the "separate" part—at least if the facilities for African-Americans and whites were "equal." At first, however, no one seemed to take the "equal" part seriously.

Three years after *Plessy* the Court had a chance to give its views. A Georgia board of education decided to close the high school it had operated for African-American students, and use the money it saved on elementary schools for younger African-Americans. African-American parents sued the school board, pointing out that it was hardly "equal" for the board to close the high school for African-Americans while keeping the high school for whites open.

Justice Harlan, the dissenter in *Plessy,* wrote the Court's opinion rejecting the challenge (*Cumming v. Board of Education,* 1899). His opinion can be read narrowly, as if it said that the parents had simply sought the wrong remedy—he thought they were asking the board to *close* the white school rather than *reopen* the African-American one. Generally, though, people took *Plessy* and later cases to allow segregation in education, and no legislature in the South ever made a serious effort to guarantee that African-American schools really were equal to the white schools.

(Racial segregation was most important in the South, but it occurred elsewhere. Mexican-American children were often segregated in the Southwest, for example. One curious case involving an Asian American who claimed that she had been unconstitutionally assigned to the school for blacks reached the Supreme Court in 1927 [*Gong Lum v. Rice,* 1927].)

African-American historian Rayford Logan called the period when *Plessy* was decided the low point in the nation's treatment of its African-American members. Early in the twentieth century the African-American community's efforts to defend itself took on new forms.

Booker T. Washington, head of Alabama's Tuskegee Institute, argued strongly that the African-American community had to make the best of the subordinated position white Americans forced on it. By training African-Americans to work hard in the lowest-paid jobs and under the worst conditions, the community could strengthen itself and eventually develop enough financial resources to lead whites to an "appreciation of [their] merits," as the Court had said in *Plessy.* Although his public statements were conciliatory, asking African-Americans to accept their conditions without protest, Washington actually worked behind the scenes to support challenges to segregation.

Washington's chief opponent within the African-American community was W. E. B. Du Bois, a brilliant and acerbic intellectual and writer who was the first African-American to receive a doctorate from Harvard University. Du Bois accepted Washington's program of strengthening the African-American community, as far as it went, but insisted that the community must also aggressively press for a transformation of race relations. To develop the community, Du Bois wanted to ensure that it would be led by what he called its "Talented

Tenth," the 10 percent at the top of the community. To transform race relations, Du Bois supported creating a new organization.

As Du Bois was urging the African-American community to adopt a more dynamic approach to transforming race relations, progressive whites were becoming concerned about the nation's apparent abandonment of the vision of racial equality. The two elements came together at the end of the century's first decade. Based on prior meetings of Du Bois's Niagara Movement, whites and African-Americans founded the National Association for the Advancement of Colored People (NAACP) in 1909.

The NAACP was the first nationwide civil rights organization that had a significant impact on race relations. It proceeded on several fronts. It developed a membership base, largely in the African-American community. (Whites tended to concentrate in the national leadership, not in the "branches" that were the NAACP's local organizations.) The NAACP hired Du Bois to edit a national magazine, *The Crisis,* which became a major forum for discussion of civil rights issues. It engaged in substantial publicity campaigns, investigating episodes in which white mobs lynched African-Americans accused or only suspected of crimes and issuing brochures and reports decrying the terrorism practiced against African-Americans. It attempted, though without much success, to lobby Congress and the executive branch to adopt better policies, such as a federal law making lynching illegal. Finally, it supported legal challenges to segregation.

One of the NAACP's earliest legal cases challenged a Jim Crow ordinance adopted in Louisville,

Kentucky, where neither African-Americans nor whites were allowed to buy property in neighborhoods with a majority of the other race (*Buchanan v. Warley*, 1917). Another important case attacked mob-dominated convictions of African-Americans (*Moore v. Dempsey*, 1926).

The legal attack on segregation was important to the NAACP because publicity, lobbying, and other forms of political pressure simply were not likely to get very far in the 1910s and 1920s. To persuade politicians to act, the NAACP had to persuade them that they could get votes by doing what the NAACP thought right. To persuade judges to act, in contrast, the NAACP "merely" had to show that the practices it challenged violated the Constitution. Judges applying the law might be more neutral and detached than politicians seeking votes.

*Plessy v. Ferguson* showed, of course, that there were no guarantees even in going to the courts. After *Plessy*, though, the Supreme Court started to show more sympathy for challenges to discrimination. It invalidated a "grandfather clause" that was part of the South's effort to make sure that only whites could vote (*Guinn v. United States*, 1915). Five justices indicated that they would take seriously the requirement that railroads really had to provide "equal" separate facilities for African-Americans (*McCabe v. Atchison, Topeka & Santa Fe Railway*, 1914). None of this did much to erode the Jim Crow system, but it held out hope that using the courts might eventually make a difference.

By the middle of the 1920s the NAACP's leaders decided that the time had come to chart a new course. The NAACP's executive director James Weldon Johnson (who was also a major poet, the author of "Lift Every Voice and Sing," known as the "black national anthem") sat on the board of a charitable foundation, the Garland Fund, which was trying to find ways to support progressive political and social groups. The fund had been created when Charles Garland, the heir to a substantial mining fortune, decided that the money was tainted with the blood of workers and that he had to give it away.

The Garland Fund gave the NAACP some grants for investigations and publicity campaigns. One series of reports published in *The Crisis* showed what "separate but equal" meant in the South's schools: In Georgia, schools spent over eight times as much for each white student as they did for each African-American; even in North Carolina, widely believed to be the "best" among the Southern states, spending on whites was twice that on African-Americans.

These reports led Johnson to develop a new proposal to the Garland Fund.[1] The NAACP asked for money to develop a legal campaign against segregation. The idea was to try to force Southern states to take "separate but equal" seriously, to increase the funding of African-American schools to a level equal to that of white schools. According to the NAACP's proposal, lawsuits to equalize spending would have three main effects. They would become the focus of public attention, and so allow the NAACP to educate the public about what the Jim Crow system really was; they would "give

---

[1]Draft Report from Max Ernst and Walter White to American Fund for Public Service, [April?] 1930, Box I-C-196, NAACP Papers, Manuscript Division, Library of Congress, cited in Mark Tushnet, *The NAACP's Legal Strategy Against Segregated Education, 1925–1950* (Chapel Hill: University of North Carolina Press, 1987), p. 14.

James Weldon Johnson, black poet and executive
director of the NAACP, who proposed that the
NAACP challenge legal segregation

courage to Negroes" by showing that the Jim Crow system really could be challenged; and they would raise the cost of segregation so high that the South would simply give up on trying to maintain separate schools that really were equal.

The Garland Fund's leaders were skeptical about the NAACP's claims, but they went along with a modest grant to develop a plan for a litigation campaign. The NAACP hired Nathan Margold, a recent graduate of Harvard Law School, to design the campaign.

The very fact that the NAACP's leaders had begun to think about a systematic litigation campaign, carefully designed to erode segregation through a series of court challenges, was more important than the details of Margold's plan, which actually never was carried out. Until the early 1930s, constitutional litigation was catch-as-catch-can, with the NAACP reacting to lynchings or new Jim Crow ordinances. Now the NAACP was prepared to go on the offensive.

# Chapter 2

# VICTORIES IN THE LOWER COURTS

Charles Hamilton Houston was the first African-American at Harvard Law School whose grades were so high that he served on the school's law review. After graduating in 1922 and traveling in Europe on a prestigious Harvard fellowship, Houston went back to his hometown, Washington, D.C., where he began to practice law with his father.

Houston also began teaching at Howard University's law school. Founded after the Civil War to provide higher education for the newly emancipated slaves, Howard was a center for African-American scholarship and activism in the 1920s. Its law school, though, was second-rate. Most of the lawyers who graduated from Howard did provide routine legal service to their African-American communities, but much of their work was slipshod, and almost none involved efforts to fight race discrimination.

Charles Hamilton Houston, the first African-American
graduate of Harvard Law School, the dean of Howard
Law School, and the lawyer who developed the
NAACP's legal strategy to fight segregation

Houston had a very different vision of what lawyers could do. Inspired by his teachers and mentors at Harvard, including Felix Frankfurter (later a Supreme Court justice), Houston believed that lawyers could be what he called "social engineers." They could use their legal skills to ensure that the society's laws promoted justice, by obtaining legal rulings that interpreted statutes and the Constitution in light of their deeper purposes. Because lawyers as social engineers were designing systems that operated in the real world, they had to know sociology and history as well as law.

Howard's president put Houston in charge of upgrading the law school. Houston took on the task enthusiastically. He forced a number of teachers out, and—believing that law schools that operated in the evening and allowed students to attend part-time could not train his social engineers—Houston turned Howard into a law school for full-time students only.

The size of Howard's classes dropped dramatically, and many of those who started the program dropped out when they discovered how rigorous Houston's teaching was. Those who remained found Houston to be an inspiring though extremely demanding teacher.

The students who graduated from Howard in the 1930s were an extraordinary group, whose impact on constitutional law was enormous. Spottswood Robinson and Oliver Hill, Barbara Johns's lawyers, were among Houston's star pupils.

Houston's true protégé, though, was Thurgood Marshall. Marshall, a native of Baltimore, couldn't attend the segregated law school at the University of Maryland, so he commuted for three years from his home to Howard Law School in Washington. Recollecting his years at Howard from his vantage point as a justice on the Supreme Court, Marshall said that every civil rights issue he had faced throughout his career as a civil rights lawyer and judge had come up in discussions with Houston and his classmates.

Houston found that his role as a teacher was not enough to satisfy his desire to use the law for social change. The NAACP's vision of strategically guided litigation fit perfectly with Houston's sense of what lawyers could do. After the Garland Fund's grant ran out and Margold left the NAACP to work in the New Deal administration of President Franklin Roosevelt, Houston decided to join the NAACP's staff in New York. He became the NAACP's first full-time staff lawyer in late 1934.

Marshall joined Houston in New York less than two years later. After graduating first in his Howard law school class (a fraction of a grade point ahead of Oliver Hill), Marshall went back to Baltimore. He struggled with a small legal practice, doing landlord-tenant cases and some criminal defense work. That wasn't the kind of law Marshall really wanted to do, though. After his first year at Howard, Marshall had come under Houston's wing. He had helped Houston and his faculty colleagues research important civil rights issues, and he had watched Houston defend an African-American named George Crawford against a murder charge in a notorious case in Virginia's hunt country (Crawford escaped the death sentence through Houston's defense). *That* was what he had become a lawyer to do.

Marshall also spent a lot of time helping the community. He took on so many clients who couldn't pay him that one judge called him the "freebie lawyer." He also helped the NAACP's local branch leaders, making speeches, traveling all over

Maryland to carry the NAACP's word, helping put out fliers advertising NAACP meetings. That was no way to make a living, and Marshall found himself falling further behind in his bills.

Houston had seen Marshall as a student, and knew that Marshall had the potential to surpass his teachers. Marshall was diligent to a fault: If Houston asked him to do some research on a particular point, Marshall would go through the case reports to pull together everything Houston wanted, and more. Marshall was also a hail-fellow-well-met sort: He could make an inspiring speech, filled with humor and good sense, and then join his audience for a relaxed discussion of the day's events. Houston saw that Marshall could become one of the African-American community's most important leaders, and thought it ridiculous that Marshall was struggling to maintain a small private practice in Baltimore.

Houston maneuvered to create a job for Marshall as his assistant in New York. Marshall wasn't sure that he wanted to leave Baltimore, and the NAACP wasn't sure that it could pay a second lawyer, so both sides agreed to try the job out for six months. Marshall stayed with the NAACP from 1936 to 1961.

When Houston got to New York in 1934, Margold had written his plan for the legal campaign against segregation. It called for a group of coordinated lawsuits seeking to equalize spending on white and African-American schools. Houston thought that Margold's plan was unrealistic. Margold's legal theory was strained, Houston believed, and actually carrying out the lawsuits would be almost impossible: There just weren't enough lawyers to file enough suits to make it too expensive to maintain segregation.

Houston had another problem with Margold's plan. Although lawyers were bound to be important in any litigation effort, Margold's plan took too much away from the local African-American communities. As Houston saw it, lawsuits were only part of the NAACP's effort to transform race relations. Vigorous local organizations had to carry out the other parts. Nothing in Margold's plan took advantage of the NAACP's branches, or did anything to give them a significant role in the lawsuits.

Houston thought there was a better way to conduct the lawsuits. Instead of focusing on total expenditures in the schools, Houston decided to focus only on teachers' salaries. The differences between what white and African-American teachers were paid were dramatic: In the 1930s when Houston took over the lawsuits, it was unusual to find African-American teachers who were paid more than half of what white teachers got, and it was not unusual to find white teachers paid four or five times as much as African-American teachers. Even in the 1940s, when school boards knew they faced legal challenges to unequal salaries, the lawsuits turned up school boards with pay scales for white teachers at various levels of experience and training, matched in the next column by a statement that African-American teachers with the same experience and training would get 75 percent of the white pay scale.

Focusing on teachers' salaries had several advantages, from Houston's point of view. The large differences made it easy to establish that "separate" actually meant "unequal." Because only money was at stake, Houston thought that school boards might resist the lawsuits less strenuously than if he challenged segregation directly. Because teachers' salaries would surely rise if they won the lawsuits, Houston could use the lawsuits as a way of showing the African-American community not only that lawsuits could make a difference, but also that the NAACP was an organization worth supporting. By strengthening the NAACP, the lawsuits would provide the basis for other forms of political action later on.

Houston added another type of case to the legal campaign. His experience at Howard showed him that talented African-Americans from all over the segregated South wanted graduate and professional training that they could not get in their home states, which—like Marshall's Maryland—operated graduate and professional schools exclusively for whites. Houston thought it worthwhile to try to get Southern states to *establish* graduate and professional programs for African-Americans. Here too winning the cases would, he thought, be easy. *Plessy* said that "separate but equal" was constitutional, but in the segregated South, graduate and professional education for African-Americans was not simply separate; it didn't even exist. Whatever *Plessy* might mean, surely it couldn't mean *that*.

Houston envisioned a second stage for the graduate and professional school cases. His experience as an educator taught him that graduate schools were not just buildings and books. Graduate education was a complex process in which students made professional contacts, got a sense of what it was like to be a professional in a community, and participated in a wide range of extracurricular but educationally important programs, like the law review on which Houston had served at Harvard.

What would happen after a Southern state created a separate graduate program for African-Americans? Houston believed that the next step would be to show that this separate program was not equal to the one available for whites, because it lacked all the intangible aspects that were so important to graduate and professional education. Southern universities would then have to desegregate. That might not be so difficult, at least compared to desegregating elementary and secondary schools, because fewer whites attended universities, and those who did probably didn't care as much about maintaining total segregation as elected school boards.

Houston and Marshall divided up the legal chores. Marshall spent most of his time on the teachers' salary cases. The NAACP lawyers brought most of the first salary cases in Maryland, where Marshall had strong ties to the teachers, the NAACP branch, and the local bench and bar. From the late 1930s to the mid-1940s, the NAACP routinely won these salary cases. Sometimes school boards were recalcitrant, which meant that cases dragged on for several years. These delays sometimes bothered the teachers, who were impatient about how long it took to get their salaries raised. The facts of the cases were so clear, and the inequalities so obvious, though, that the victories rolled in.

By 1945 the salary cases had gone about as far as they could. Although his permanent office was in New York, Marshall spent a lot of time on the road, investigating the facts about teachers' salaries in different school districts all over the South. Of course, Marshall used these trips to build the NAACP as an organization, and he became one of the NAACP's most highly regarded speakers as a result.

Getting the salary cases in shape, though, took a lot of lawyer time, which Marshall had less and less of. The NAACP's staff gradually expanded, but by 1945 there still were only two or three lawyers on the staff available to work on the legal campaign. Basically, the staff could handle cases only from the South's largest cities, and by 1945 it had won those cases. The time had come to move to the next stage of the legal campaign.

The problem with the graduate and professional school cases was different. Teachers all over the South wanted to increase their salaries, and there were a lot of teachers willing to sign up as plaintiffs in the lawsuits. The graduate and professional cases involved fewer—and younger—people, who had recently graduated from college. They wanted an education. As some of the cases involving teachers' salaries showed, lawsuits can take a while. Universities came up with all sorts of delaying tactics, demanding lots of documents from the plaintiffs and the NAACP. They were also able to use their power in the community to harass plaintiffs: Some plaintiffs found their draft boards particularly interested in seeing that they got into the military quickly, while others lost their jobs. Delays and harassment meant that Houston and Marshall found it hard to keep the lawsuits against universities going.

Houston won the legal campaign's first Supreme Court victory in 1938. Lloyd Gaines, the president of the senior class at his black college, wanted to be a lawyer. With the NAACP's assistance, he applied to the segregated University of Missouri Law School, which of course turned him down. Under state law, though, the university had to offer him a scholarship to pay his way at law school in neighboring Iowa. That didn't satisfy him, because an important part of education at a state law school is getting to know just how local judges and lawyers react to different styles of being a lawyer.

Missouri gave Gaines another choice: If he asked, the state's segregated university for African-Americans would *create* a law school. Houston knew that this choice opened the way for the next step in the legal campaign, a challenge to separate graduate programs as unequal. He took Gaines's case to the Supreme Court, which ruled for Gaines. The out-of-state scholarship didn't satisfy the requirement that the state offer at least a separate law program for African-Americans. Merely *offering* to create a law school wasn't enough either: Missouri actually had to create one as soon as Gaines applied.

That turned out to be a real problem. Missouri's legislature appropriated $200,000 for new graduate programs at the segregated university for African-Americans. Gaines, though, never attended. He simply disappeared; Houston and Marshall tried to track him down, and they heard rumors that he had moved to Mexico, or that he had been murdered, but they never found out what had happened to him. Over the next few years Houston tried to desegregate Missouri's journalism program, but the university managed to obstruct him there too: As its last move, the university simply shut down the graduate journalism program for whites, saying that World War II had reduced enrollments so much that it didn't make sense to keep the program going.

Houston left the NAACP's national office in 1938, returning to Washington to practice law with his father, who had always insisted that Houston try to keep up a general legal practice that could support him and his family once the fight against race discrimination was won. Marshall took over as the leader of the legal campaign, a role he held through the Supreme Court's decision in *Brown v. Board of Education*.

The end of World War II opened up new opportunities for the legal effort. African-Americans who had served in the armed forces returned home to find that, although they had fought a war to preserve democracy elsewhere in the world, they remained a downtrodden people in the United States. More and more African-Americans were willing to step forward to help the legal effort, as plaintiffs and community organizers.

Marshall faced pressure from within the NAACP, and from his staff, to move ahead quickly in a challenge to segregated education from elementary schools upward. He hesitated, believing that the South would resist desegregation unless the courts made it absolutely clear that segregation was unconstitutional. Marshall was concerned that the groundwork for such a decision really hadn't been laid. All he had in hand were some lower-court decisions in salary cases, and the single Supreme Court decision in the Gaines case. He needed more.

As Marshall saw it, Houston's strategy of challenging the supposed "equality" of separate facilities should still be followed. Southern governors, responding to the salary cases and to their lawyers' advice that they could not maintain grossly unequal facilities indefinitely, began to ask their legislatures to spend money upgrading African-American schools. They also made feeble efforts to create separate graduate programs.

Marshall continued to follow Houston's path. A Texas mail carrier named Heman Sweatt—whom Marshall called a perfect client except that journalists always misspelled his name as Herman— wanted to become a clerk, but his postmaster discriminated against African-Americans. An activist in the NAACP, Sweatt decided that this experience showed how important it was for African-Americans to go to law school, and he applied to the University of Texas Law School. Of course, it rejected his application, but the state did actually create a law school for African-Americans.

Marshall seized the chance to take the next step, arguing that the new law school could not possibly be "equal" to the one whites attended. The state appropriated money for a law school in Houston—now known as the Texas Southern University Thurgood Marshall School of Law—but in the meantime set up a tiny operation in a basement across the street from the state capitol in Austin. Teachers from the white school, also in Austin, were assigned to teach some of the classes; because of opposition from the African-American community, though, enrollment was so low that the Austin law school never really went into operation.

Sweatt's case reached the Supreme Court in 1950. The only record the Court possessed was a description of the makeshift operation in Austin, which no one could seriously think was equal to the long-established and well-financed University of Texas Law School.

Unknown to Marshall, he had a strong ally on the Supreme Court: Texan Tom Clark. Clark had been attorney general before Harry Truman appointed him to the Court in 1949, and liberal supporters of the NAACP were suspicious of Clark's views on race because of his background. They were wrong. When the justices discussed Sweatt's case, Clark told them that it was ridiculous to think that the new school for African-Americans could equal the school for whites, which was "a professional school of top rank." Clark pointed out to his colleagues the important place the University of Texas Law School had in the

Supreme Court justice Tom Clark of Texas shared
Marshall's view that the separate schools for African-
Americans were not equal to the schools for whites.

social and legal network of the Texas bar, and said that no new school could possibly have a similar place.

Sweatt's case got to the Supreme Court along with two others. One involved the University of Oklahoma's graduate program in education. The state didn't have *any* graduate programs for African-Americans, which made their legal position completely impossible. George McLaurin got a court order directing the university to admit him, which it did. Instead of treating him like an ordinary student, however, the university tried to segregate McLaurin inside the school: The classes he enrolled in were rescheduled to meet in a room that had an alcove on the side, and the university required McLaurin to sit in the alcove. (Eventually it relented a little, and let him sit in a separate row in the classroom, barring anyone else from sitting in that row.)

The facts in McLaurin's case could hardly have been better at showing how segregation was designed to humiliate African-Americans. And the facts in Sweatt's case, though not quite as powerful, went a long way toward showing that separate graduate programs could never be equal.

The third case the Court had to decide was somewhat less dramatic, but it had a major impact on the Court. Elmer Henderson was an African-American employed by the federal government to investigate employment discrimination. On one of his trips to the South, Henderson tried to get service in his train's dining car. The railroad ordinarily reserved two tables, separate from the rest, for its African-American riders, but it would seat whites at those tables if there were no other places. When Henderson got to the dining car, whites were eating at the "reserved" tables, and the railroad refused to let Henderson occupy the one vacant seat.

Henderson charged the railroad with discrimination before the federal Interstate Commerce Commission. The Commission ruled against him, and Henderson took his case to the Supreme Court. When the case got to the Court, the United States Department of Justice came down on *Henderson's* side, even though formally he was suing the ICC, a federal agency.

The government's position carried a lot of weight within the Supreme Court. Marshall pressed two claims on the Court in *Sweatt* and *McLaurin*. First, he said, the states were not complying with the requirement of "separate but equal" because neither the Texas makeshift law school nor the humiliating conditions imposed on McLaurin provided equal educational opportunities. But, Marshall continued, *Plessy* should be overruled, because segregation violated the basic rule of racial equality embodied in the Fourteenth Amendment. The Department of Justice took the same position.

The Court ruled against segregation in all three cases, but it said that it didn't have to decide the "broader issues" raised by Marshall and the Justice Department. Chief Justice Fred Vinson, a Kentuckian, wrote in Sweatt's case that the separate law school could not offer African-Americans "substantial equality in . . . educational opportunities." Following Clark's lead, the opinion emphasized the social contacts students made during law school, their exposure to a wide range of students from varied backgrounds, and other "intangible" aspects of a legal education. McLaurin's case was even easier. The restrictions the university imposed "handicapped" McLaurin by making it harder for him to study and "to engage in discussions and exchange views with other students." (The Court decided in Henderson's favor by finding that the railroad's actions violated a federal statute, and didn't say anything about the Constitution.)

Vinson's opinions in *Sweatt* and *McLaurin* were hardly eloquent attacks on the very idea of segregation. They were, however, of enormous legal significance, which Marshall grasped as soon as he read them. Southern states were trying hard to upgrade the segregated elementary and secondary schools for African-Americans; even Barbara Johns's school board in Prince Edward County had promised to build a new high school pretty soon.

If these building programs were carried out, it might have been quite hard for Marshall and his NAACP lawyers to show that they were "unequal" to the white schools in any material sense: They would be newer than many of the schools for whites, for example, and might well have at least some better-equipped laboratories and the like. No matter what the new schools were like, challenging them as unequal in the material sense—comparing their "bricks and mortar" to what the white schools had—would have been an incredibly costly and time-consuming task, far worse than the problems posed by the later teachers' salary cases.

When the Court emphasized the intangible aspects of education in *Sweatt* and *McLaurin*—the opportunities for social contacts, the importance of learning from other students with different backgrounds—it made it possible for Marshall to redirect the focus of challenges to segregated elemen-

Supreme Court chief justice Fred Vinson's opinions on segregation were of enormous legal significance.

tary and secondary education. Instead of showing that the buildings in any particular district were not equal, he could try to show that segregated education could *never* be equal in these intangible but truly important ways.

# Chapter 3

# DESIGNING A FULL-SCALE ATTACK ON SEGREGATION

As soon as the Court announced its decisions in *Sweatt* and *McLaurin,* Marshall knew that he had to start the full-scale attack on segregation. That meant locating cases and getting them ready for trial, but for the attack to succeed he had to get his cases to the Supreme Court.

In 1950, when the full-scale attack began, the Supreme Court had gone through a decade of change. From the early 1900s through 1937 the Court had been a steadfast supporter of conservative politics. Invoking the general "due process" clause of the Fourteenth Amendment, the Court said that minimum wage and maximum hours laws were unconstitutional; it used other constitutional provisions to obstruct other parts of the agenda that liberals pushed through legislatures.

Franklin Roosevelt, elected in 1932 in the middle of the nation's worst depression in decades, thought that the power of government could solve the nation's problems. His New Deal legislative program created a host of new federal agencies, and exercised national power more extensively than ever before.

The Supreme Court stood in Roosevelt's way, however. Led by four conservatives who managed to pick up an additional vote or two in nearly every case, the Court held major parts of Roosevelt's New Deal program unconstitutional. Roosevelt reacted by proposing what came to be known as his "Court-packing" plan, which would have allowed him to add up to six more justices to the Supreme Court. The plan was defeated, but the Court got the message.

After 1937 the Court's membership changed completely, and the justices developed a theory that explained why they should look out for the interests of African-Americans.

The justices who sat on the Court in the early 1950s had been appointed by Presidents Roosevelt and Truman. Some, like Hugo Black, who as senator from Alabama was a leader in pressing forward the New Deal agenda, had been prominent politicians. Chief Justice Fred Vinson had been Truman's secretary of the treasury after working in several wartime federal agencies. Even the justices who are obscure today were prominent at the time: Harold Burton, for example, had been mayor of Cleveland and senator from Ohio before his appointment to the Court.

The justices' political experience, and their commitment to the political program of the Roosevelt-Truman Democratic party, made them sensitive to the issues in the segregation cases. They understood that Southerners had been important supporters of the Democratic party's progressive eco-

Supreme Court justice Hugo Black, a Southerner and a liberal, was sensitive to the issues in the segregation cases.

nomic programs, and Hugo Black at least was concerned that Supreme Court rulings against segregation might destroy the liberal wing of the party in the South for a generation or more.

They also understood, though, that other parts of the Democratic coalition deeply opposed segregation. Roosevelt's economic recovery programs pulled the African-American community away from its traditional affiliation with the Republican party of Abraham Lincoln. As African-Americans continued to migrate to the North, they changed states that had been solidly Republican into states the Democrats had a chance to win, if the Democrats appealed to African-Americans and their interests.

The intellectual and cultural climate changed too. In 1944 the Swedish sociologist Gunnar Myrdal published *An American Dilemma,* a study that pointed out the tension between the nation's ideological commitment to equality and the perpetuation of legal segregation in the South. This situation, Myrdal argued, couldn't last much longer. Myrdal's book symbolized the complete erosion of any intellectual defense of segregation. Equally symbolic, but of real cultural importance, in 1947 Jackie Robinson became the first African-American to play in major league baseball.

The convergence of all these factors made it likely that some transformation of the nation's race relations would occur in the 1950s. In 1947 President Truman appointed a commission to report on civil rights, and he endorsed its recommendations for a strong civil rights program. In 1948 Truman signed an order starting the process of desegregating the armed forces. These actions seemed to make Truman vulnerable politically. Southern Democrats, led by South Carolina's governor Strom Thurmond, walked out of the party's nominating convention in 1948, and Thurmond ran against Truman in the 1948 presidential election. Truman's political instincts were sound, however; he won the election by re-creating the New Deal coalition of liberals, union members, and African-Americans.

All this meant that the political and cultural climate was ripe for change. Could the Supreme Court have any significant role? The Court's reaction to the New Deal crisis might have suggested that the Court would stay away from controversial political issues like race relations. In a series of decisions beginning in 1937 the Court remade constitutional law. It endorsed expansive definitions of national power, allowing Congress to exercise its constitutional power to regulate interstate commerce in nearly any way it wanted. The Court also repeatedly stated that legislatures should be given a lot of room to develop policies they thought wise. According to the Court after the New Deal, courts should find laws unconstitutional only rarely. By developing this theory of judicial restraint in the face of legislative choices, the Court seemed to have abandoned the kind of activism that Marshall and the NAACP wanted from it.

The Court's theory of judicial restraint did not mean, though, that it would *never* find laws unconstitutional. In one crucial case, the Court used a footnote to suggest some limits on how far it would go in letting legislatures do what they wanted. In traditional civil liberties cases, the Court said, it would take the words of the Constitution seriously. Even more, where laws discriminated against what it called "discrete and insular minorities," who might not have enough political power to get a legislature's attention, the Court said that *it* would take care to enforce the minority's rights.[2]

With this theory in hand, the Court *could* rule in Marshall's favor—if he gave the justices the right cases and the right legal theories.

Getting the cases was fairly easy for Marshall. African-Americans all over the country were as fed up as Barbara Johns. In the late 1940s students in Lumberton, North Carolina, in Hearne, Texas, and in South Park, Kansas, walked out of school to protest the run-down segregated schools they had to attend. In Kansas, NAACP branches in Wichita and Topeka competed for the honor of supporting a lawsuit challenging their state's segregation statute.

Topeka won the competition. Elisha Scott and his sons, African-American lawyers active in the NAACP, met Oliver Brown, a railroad welder whose daughter Linda had a dangerous walk across railroad tracks and a main street to get to her school bus. At first they wanted simply a better transportation system to get the children to the segregated schools. Brown quickly decided, though, that challenging segregation itself was more important.

At about the same time in South Carolina, Reverend Joseph DeLaine heard an NAACP officer give a speech about segregation, mentioning the NAACP's desire to support a lawsuit where white children rode to school while African-American children had to walk. That described DeLaine's hometown, Summerton, South Carolina, and

[2]United States v. Carolene Products Co., 304 U.S. 144, 152–53 n. 4 (1938).

DeLaine started to organize Summerton parents to petition the school board for buses. The parents had gotten together to buy their own bus, but it broke down a lot, and they needed better transportation for their children.

Marshall went to South Carolina and met in secret with DeLaine—NAACP supporters in the deep South always feared that whites would fire them from their jobs, or worse, if their membership became known—and persuaded DeLaine to shift his focus from the school buses to segregation itself. DeLaine decided to go ahead with a direct challenge to segregation.

DeLaine began to organize meetings at local churches, and as his efforts became known to the white community, retaliation started. Harry Briggs, an auto mechanic whose name appeared first on the lawsuit that eventually was filed, lost his job, and farmers who signed on to the lawsuit found it hard to get credit to buy supplies for their farms.

Parents in two Delaware school districts also complained to the NAACP. In one district the parents had to send their children to a segregated high school miles away, when there was a white high school in the neighborhood, and they didn't like that. In the other, a school bus taking white children to school went right past one African-American student's house and then went by her school, but she had to walk to school anyway.

In Washington, D.C., overcrowding at a junior high school was the problem. Space was available at a nearby white school, and eleven African-American students applied for admission. Of course they were turned down. Houston got behind the legal challenge to segregation, and from his "death bed" (as another lawyer put it), directed the

Mrs. Daisy Bates, president of the Arkansas chapter of
the NAACP, and Robert Carter, NAACP staff lawyer and
assistant to Thurgood Marshall, in court

case to James Nabrit, who worked closely with the NAACP's staff lawyers on the challenge.

By 1950 Marshall had a somewhat larger staff to work with; he could call on four or five permanent staff members: Robert Carter, his chief assistant; Jack Greenberg, who was to follow Marshall as the staff's chief lawyer in 1961; Constance Baker Motley—like Carter, later a federal judge; and a few others—along with dedicated lawyers in the states where the lawsuits were filed such as Oliver Hill, Spottswood Robinson, James Nabrit, and Elisha Scott. He divided the staff into several units, each devoted to one of the cases, and deployed them across the country.

The cases, along with Barbara Johns's from Virginia, presented several legal variations on the basic theme that segregation was unconstitutional, but the legal variations were less important than the political ones. The cases from South Carolina and Virginia came from the heart of segregated society, while the ones from Delaware and Kansas came from border states where segregation, while strongly entrenched, was not nearly as important a part of the overall social and political culture. The case from Washington made the point that segregation was a national embarrassment: In the nation's capital city, where politicians raged against the lack of democracy in the Soviet Union and elsewhere behind the Iron Curtain, the laws created a caste society.

Marshall faced something of a dilemma as these cases developed. He represented both his clients and his cause. His ethical obligations meant that, no matter how much he cared for his cause, he had to make sure that pursuing the attack on segregation didn't prevent his clients from getting the better schools they wanted for their children.

One part of the legal attack was easy. If Marshall and his staff showed that the *material* conditions in the segregated schools were unequal—that the high school in Delaware didn't have science labs, or that bus transportation in Topeka was inadequate, for example—they would "win" the cases, because *Plessy* required that separate schools be equal. That kind of victory wasn't enough for Marshall, though. States could respond to it by putting more money into the segregated schools, while continuing the segregation *system*. Still, because Marshall's clients would actually get better schools as a result, he had to include challenges to material conditions in his lawsuits.

In fact, while the South Carolina case was working its way through the courts, South Carolina's governor, James M. Byrnes, who had been a Supreme Court justice briefly in the early 1940s, pushed through a special appropriations bill designed to thwart challenges to segregation by creating a building fund to upgrade the segregated schools for African-Americans. Marshall was pretty confident that, in the long run, he and his lawyers could show that even with more money invested, the segregated schools would still not be equal in material terms to the white schools. But, if all Marshall did was "win" the cases by getting the courts to take the "equal" part of "separate but equal" seriously, no one would have been satisfied. The NAACP lacked the resources to litigate "inequality" cases all over the South, and in any case the constitutionality of segregated institutions—equal or unequal—would not be the issue.

The 1950 university cases raised the hopes of African-Americans, who pressed Marshall to attack segregation directly. The university cases offered a legal theory to challenge segregation itself. They emphasized the intangible aspects of education. Some, like the availability of a law review and the importance of a network of alumni for lawyers in practice, were limited to the professional setting. Others, though, also arose in elementary and secondary schools; children, no less than prospective lawyers, were deprived of opportunities to learn from people of diverse backgrounds when they were confined to segregated schools, for example.

What Marshall needed here was some "hook" to show that children were harmed by the very fact of segregation, no matter how well equipped the schools they attended were. Robert Carter came up with the hook. He called a psychologist from Columbia University who directed him to Kenneth Clark, a graduate student who had done some research with his wife on the image African-American children had of themselves. In their research, the Clarks showed children a number of dolls, some white, some dark, and asked them which was the nicest doll, which the ugliest, and which was most like themselves. The Clarks' research showed that African-American children typically called the white dolls nice and the dark ones ugly, while saying that the dark ones were most like themselves. According to the Clarks, this showed that African-American children had negative self-images.

Kenneth Clark gave the doll tests to children in the South Carolina case, and testified in the Virginia and Kansas cases as well. His evidence was not tremendously compelling, though. It turned out that African-American children in the North gave roughly the same answers that children in the segregated South gave. That made it hard to say that the children had negative self-

Kenneth Clark, African-American psychologist who
testified for the NAACP on the injurious effects of
segregation on children

images because of *segregation* rather than, say, the overall conditions of the races in the United States. No one involved in the lawsuits thought that this evidence was really crucial to their cases. For them it was just another bit of evidence showing that something was rotten with the segregation system. Later, though, the Supreme Court's critics focused on what they described as the silly doll tests that they thought had persuaded the Court to strike segregation down.

For the lawyers, the trials in the segregation cases were routine. There were few dramatic moments, no aggressive cross-examinations that revealed anything the lawyers hadn't known before. The South Carolina trial, however, was an important civic event. Marshall was a charismatic figure in the African-American community, which often greeted his appearances in town with enormous fervor. He took charge of the South Carolina case, and African-Americans lined the courthouse steps to get in to hear Marshall at work. After Marshall examined one state witness named Crow—who was in charge of supervising Governor Byrnes's school construction program—one African-American listener said gleefully that Marshall "sure loves to eat crow."[3]

All of the cases except the one in Delaware were filed in federal court, and three of those were heard by special three-judge courts, with no juries. Delaware was different, too, because the state court judges ruled in *favor* of the African-American plaintiffs. The trial judge actually went to see the schools in the two districts, and he concluded that

---

[3]Quoted from Tinsley Yarbrough, *A Passion for Justice: J. Waties Waring and Civil Rights* (New York: Oxford University Press, 1987), pp. 184–85.

segregation itself led to inferior education. The state supreme court agreed.

Elsewhere the lower courts ruled against the plaintiffs. The South Carolina court had on it one dedicated segregationist, but its major figures were John Parker and J. Waties Waring. Herbert Hoover had nominated Judge Parker for a seat on the Supreme Court in 1930, but the Senate rejected the nomination after a campaign against him led by labor unions and the NAACP. Parker was one of the nation's most respected judges; careful and cautious, he was regarded as a racial moderate by the 1950s, which meant that he was unlikely to do much to change the segregation system. The third South Carolina judge, though, was different. Judge Waring was a vigorous liberal. His inclinations against segregation were reinforced by his second wife, who had been raised in New York. The Warings' views on race made them social outcasts among South Carolina's white elite.

Judge Waring received some of the preliminary papers in the South Carolina case, and he reportedly was shocked that the NAACP apparently was not trying to get rid of segregation entirely, but seemed to be challenging only limited aspects of Summerton's school bus system. Waring told Marshall to refile the case as a total challenge to segregation. As a result, the case came before the three-judge court.

The case almost got derailed at the last moment. Summerton's lawyer opened the trial with a statement conceding that the African-American schools were grossly inferior to the white schools as far as the material, brick-and-mortar conditions were concerned. He asked the court for time to correct the situation, to get the system in line with the "separate but equal" rule. The lawyer's concession disrupted Marshall's plans for the trial. He had lined up a number of witnesses who were to testify about conditions in the schools. Marshall scrambled to present Clark's testimony, which Carter followed up during a second day of trial. But that was basically all the evidence there was—or, really, needed to be.

Judge Parker wrote the court's opinion, which came out in June 1951. Because of the lawyer's concession about inequality of facilities, Parker told the board to come back in six months and report on the improvements it had made in the facilities. That simply followed *Plessy v. Ferguson*. Parker's opinion rejected all the broader claims Marshall had presented. Segregation in elementary schools, Parker wrote, was different from segregation in professional schools because of the importance of professional contacts at the higher level.

He ended by referring indirectly to what everyone knew was the real issue that made the segregation cases difficult. The Constitution might be interpreted to bar segregation, but the white South was unlikely to accept such a ruling readily. As Parker put it, "If public education is to have the support of the people, . . . it must not go contrary to what they deem for the best interests of their children." The attack on segregation, Parker said, was based on "sociological" ideas, and judges "have no more right to read their ideas of sociology into the Constitution than their ideas of economics."

Judge Waring wrote a passionate dissent. He said that segregation rested on "sophistry and prejudice," and that the Supreme Court had gradually come to understand that segregation violated the Constitution. Marshall's expert witnesses, Waring wrote, demonstrated that "the mere fact of segregation, itself, had a deleterious and warping effect upon the minds of children." He concluded, "Segregation is per se inequality."

Parker's distinction between law and sociology continued to bedevil the courts as they grappled with the segregation cases. Although the three judges who heard the Topeka case at the trial level ruled unanimously against the Browns, they tried to set the case up for Supreme Court review by making two findings that supported the Browns' claim. First, they agreed with Jack Greenberg, who tried the case for the NAACP, that conditions in the Topeka schools were not that dramatically unequal (again considering only physical conditions), and found as a fact that the conditions were

Segregated school in Georgia

63

actually equal. Greenberg had put more emphasis in the trial on the psychological effects of segregation, and on the importance of elementary education in shaping a student's entire life and outlook. Here too the judges agreed. Their second key factual finding was that segregation "has a detrimental effect upon the colored children," which is "greater when it has the sanction of law." Segregation, the judges found, produces "a sense of inferiority [that] affects the motivation of a child to learn." Although sympathetic to the challenge to segregation, the judges in Oklahoma left it to the Supreme Court to overrule *Plessy*.

Today the Supreme Court hears only the cases it wants to. In the early 1950s the rules were different. The Court had to hear cases decided by three-judge courts like those in South Carolina and Oklahoma. Not that this really mattered to the justices. After the 1950 university cases everyone knew that the Court was going to have to face up to the question of segregation in elementary and secondary schools. In fact, Justice Tom Clark had referred directly to that question in explaining his vote in the Texas law school case. He didn't think that the Court actually had to *decide* the question about elementary schools in 1950, although he admitted that what the Court said in the university cases was going to have some implications for that question. "If some say this undermines *Plessy*," Clark wrote his colleagues, "then let it fall. . . ."[4]

[4]Quoted from Dennis Hutchinson, "Unanimity and Desegregation: Decision Making in the Supreme Court, 1948–1958," *Georgetown Law Journal* 68 (Oct. 1979): 1, at pp. 89–90.

The only problem was that the cases got to the Court too fast, and in no particular order. Both Marshall and the justices would have liked to have more control over how the cases were presented, but only the justices had the power to assert control. Justice Felix Frankfurter, who was to play a crucial role inside the Court, told some of the Court's law clerks that the justices didn't want to decide the cases before the 1952 elections, so that the Court's action wouldn't become an issue in the fall campaigns. Actually, the justices managed to delay a decision until May 1954.

The Supreme Court considers cases in several stages. The justices decide whether to hear a case, and then set up a schedule for the ones it chooses. That schedule tells lawyers when they have to file their briefs, which provide the Court with written arguments about the case's facts, its legal issues, and the arguments the lawyers have for their side's positions. After the briefs are filed with the Court, the justices listen to oral arguments, in which the lawyers discuss the cases with the justices. Sometimes oral arguments are routine and boring—some of the arguments in the segregation cases got bogged down in endless factual detail— but sometimes they reveal what's really involved more dramatically than the written briefs. Oral arguments matter, too, because some justices learn better from hearing someone make an argument than they do from reading the same argument in a brief.

The South Carolina case got to the Court first, in the summer of 1951. By the time the justices got around to deciding what to do with the case, the school board had filed the report Judge Parker had asked for. Attempting to delay a decision, the Supreme Court then sent the case back to Judge

Parker's court, to get its "views" on what the report meant. As Justices Black and William O. Douglas said at the time, there really was no legal justification for delay, because the report was "wholly irrelevant to the constitutional questions" about whether segregation could ever be constitutional.[5] The only effect was delay. After Judge Parker's court reaffirmed its earlier decision, Marshall took the case back to the Supreme Court in May 1952.

The Topeka case came next, and it was harder to handle. Although the appeal had reached the Supreme Court in the fall of 1951, the justices simply sat on it until June 1952, when they voted to hear it, along with the South Carolina case, in October 1952. The strategy of delay had worked; the Court couldn't possibly decide the cases before the fall elections.

In the fall the justices also voted to hear the Virginia case. More revealingly, they issued an unusual order noting the existence of the District of Columbia case and inviting the plaintiffs to file an accelerated request for review. Having added these two cases to the package, the justices then postponed arguments from October to December. The Delaware case got to the Court in November, and by now the justices thought they were ready to get a handle on the entire issue. They forced the lawyers in the Delaware case to get ready for argument in December, only a few weeks away. (During the arguments, the lawyers for Delaware apologized that they couldn't refer to their briefs, which hadn't been printed in time.)

The stage was set for the Court's consideration of the constitutionality of segregation.

[5]Briggs v. Elliott, 342 U.S. 350 (1952) (Black and Douglas, JJ., dissenting).

# Chapter 4
# THE LEGAL PROBLEM

Thurgood Marshall was one of the greatest oral advocates in Supreme Court history. He could change the tone of his voice when he sarcastically described his opponent's position; he could explain how what might seem to be a complex argument actually reflected sound common sense. His greatest strengths, though, were the moral force he brought to the positions he asserted, and the conversational tone he used in most of his presentations to the Court. Segregation rested on the claim that African-Americans were fundamentally inferior to whites, Marshall always seemed to be saying, but if you just look at me you'll have to agree that that's a silly position.

Marshall expected that the justices on the Court in 1952 would *want* to rule in his favor. The political and cultural world they lived in would incline them toward his position. Chief Justice

Vinson and Tom Clark were Southerners, but Vinson had written the university cases, and Clark had been part of Harry Truman's administration when it came down on the side of civil rights. Justices Black and Douglas were probably the Court's most consistent liberals. Justice Harold Burton, although not a great legal scholar, was regarded as one of the most decent people in Washington, who took great pride in his support for civil rights as mayor of Cleveland.

Marshall's problem, then, was not to get the justices on his side, but to convince them that the law—as well as their personal views—required ruling against segregation. The two justices most concerned about distinguishing between "mere political views" and "the law" were Robert Jackson and Felix Frankfurter. Both had been deeply involved in what Jackson called the struggle against the old Court, the Court that had obstructed Roosevelt's New Deal programs. Jackson had argued in favor of New Deal statutes as Roosevelt's solicitor general, the government's chief lawyer in the Supreme Court, and then as attorney general. As a Harvard Law School professor, Frankfurter had been a close adviser to Roosevelt, particularly on legal and constitutional matters. As they worked out theories to explain why the old Court was wrong, Jackson and Frankfurter concluded that the Supreme Court had to distinguish sharply between political judgments, which had to be left to legislatures, and law, which was for the Court to decide.

Of course, the attack on segregation took the *form* of a legal argument: Marshall and his colleagues said that the Fourteenth Amendment, properly interpreted, banned segregation. What went into that interpretation, though?

When interpreting the Constitution, lawyers

Supreme Court justices Felix Frankfurter (left) and Robert Jackson (below) were concerned about distinguishing between political views and the law.

ordinarily pay attention to the Constitution's text, its history, and the judicial decisions already interpreting it. None of these were particularly strong for Marshall. The Fourteenth Amendment did have the equal protection clause, which clearly endorsed some principle of equality. It just as clearly allowed governments to treat some people differently from others, however.

The real question therefore was whether Southern states could *justify* segregation. *Plessy v. Ferguson* said that they could, if the different treatment was reasonable. This emphasis on "reasonableness" had also become part of the legal theory endorsed by New Dealers like Frankfurter and Jackson. As they saw it, the old Court had gone wrong by overturning laws that legislatures reasonably thought were sensible ways to handle social and economic problems.

The Supreme Court had suggested a different approach in a now-notorious decision during World War II. Supposedly because the military feared sabotage on the West Coast, but actually because of widespread racism, the armed forces established "internment camps" for Japanese Americans. They were forced to leave their homes on the West Coast and were relocated inland, under terrible conditions. Fred Korematsu challenged the constitutionality of the relocation program. When the Supreme Court considered his challenge in 1944, Justice Black's opinion for the Court did say that "all legal restrictions which curtail the civil rights of a single racial group are immediately suspect," and "courts must subject them to the most rigid scrutiny." Even so, the Court found that the urgent wartime conditions justified the internment program and rejected Korematsu's claim.

The doctrine the Court created in *Korematsu,* now known as "strict scrutiny," promised to help

Marshall substantially, even though the Court's bottom line in that case was that the internment camps were constitutional (because the nation was at war). Marshall could argue that segregation limited civil rights and segregation's legal restrictions could not survive the "rigid scrutiny" the Court was obligated to perform. In Korematsu's case, the Court had said as well that "racial antagonism" could never justify different treatment. What else, Marshall would ask, was the reason for segregation?

Marshall could therefore make something of the Constitution's text, and he could use recent cases—*Korematsu* and the 1950 university cases—to undermine *Plessy v. Ferguson*. History, however, was more troublesome. Justice Brown had correctly noted in *Plessy* that school segregation was widely endorsed when the Fourteenth Amendment was adopted. The very Congress that proposed the amendment to the states for adoption created a system of segregated public schools in the District of Columbia, which was especially embarrassing to the lawyers who had to argue against segregation there. When Marshall asked volunteer lawyers to look into the history of the Fourteenth Amendment, the picture became even more bleak. They discovered that virtually every time schools were mentioned during the debates over the amendment, proponents and opponents agreed that it would allow governments to operate segregated schools. Segregation in the schools was one of the routine examples of the sort of "social right" that would not be affected by the amendment.

Here too Marshall had a narrow way out. History professors John Hope Franklin and Alfred Kelly gave Marshall the idea of turning attention away from the particular ideas about segregated schools that the framers of the Fourteenth Amendment had, and toward their more general theories about civil and social rights. As another historian Marshall consulted put it, the historical argument should focus on "the overall spirit of humanitarianism, racial equalitarianism, and social idealism" that dominated those who favored the Fourteenth Amendment.

That "spirit" might explain why *Plessy* was wrongly decided and should be overruled. Humanitarianism and egalitarianism meant that governments should treat people equally in important areas of life. Public education might not have been that important in 1868, when the Fourteenth Amendment was adopted, but it had become fundamental by the 1950s. Even more, perhaps the framers—and even the justices who decided *Plessy*—might have sincerely believed that separate facilities could be equal, but experience had shown, Marshall could argue, that "separate" could never be "equal."

Marshall faced one other problem. A long line of cases, and basic ideas about constitutional rights, described constitutional rights as "personal and present." That is, if the government violated your constitutional rights, *you* are entitled to some remedy, and you should get the remedy *right away.* What else could it mean to have a constitutional right? If Marshall convinced the Supreme Court that segregation denied the students' constitutional rights, the remedy seemed obvious: a court order directing that they be allowed to attend a desegregated school.

Defining what a "desegregated school" was turned out to be more difficult than anyone thought in 1952. Marshall's problem was more immediate, though. Several justices thought that, if the Court invalidated segregation, it should give the South some time to adjust to the new system.

They were concerned that Southern whites would simply not accept a ruling that required them to admit large numbers of African-American children to the previously white schools.

That might not happen in Topeka or even many Southern cities. African-Americans and whites often lived in separate neighborhoods, and cities could get rid of segregation by law, assign children to the schools in their neighborhoods, and still keep the races separate in large measure. In districts including Summerton, South Carolina, and Prince Edward County, Virginia, that wasn't possible. Housing in rural areas wasn't segregated, and high schools were often "consolidated," drawing students from large areas. Desegregating the rural South meant having large numbers of white and African-American children in the same schools.

Neither Marshall nor his clients were concerned about satisfying the white South's nervousness about desegregation. If they won their constitutional case, they had the law on their side, and the remedy should be immediate desegregation. Marshall's problem was that some justices didn't want that to happen.

During the oral argument in Barbara Johns's case, Virginia's attorney general Lindsay Almond showed why. In an almost direct threat to the Court's authority, Almond told the justices that a desegregation decision "would destroy the public school system" because "the people would not vote bond issues through their resentment to it," and African-American teachers "would not be employed to teach white children in a tax-supported system." White resistance to desegregation might reduce the Court's order to words written in Washington with no effects in the South, and the justices could not have thought that was a desirable outcome.

If Marshall pressed too hard for immediate

desegregation, he might frighten the justices away from finding segregation unconstitutional. Somehow, the Court had to be given a way of requiring *gradual* desegregation.

Supreme Court oral arguments typically combine statements by the advocates with questions from the justices. The justices' questions to Marshall and his colleagues focused on precedent (how could they overrule as well-established a decision as *Plessy*?) and gradualism (how could they develop a remedy that delayed admission of African-American children to the previously white schools?).

The NAACP lawyers tried to explain that *Plessy* wasn't really relevant, because it involved segregation on a railroad, and that no Supreme Court case had actually ever affirmatively approved segregated education. Both points were formally correct, but the justices weren't buying them. More promising was the argument that times had changed. Justice Burton made the point: "[W]ithin seventy-five years [since *Plessy*] the social and economic conditions and the personal relations of the nation may have changed, so that what might have been a valid interpretation . . . seventy-five years ago would not be a valid interpretation . . . today."

History presented the NAACP with another problem, the approval of segregation when the Fourteenth Amendment was adopted. Marshall tried to minimize the importance of that approval, saying that things were "in a state of flux," with "the legislatures of the states at those times . . . trying to work out their problems as best they could understand." With greater understanding in 1952, different solutions were required. Marshall also placed that point within a "broader" framework, referring to the more recent university cases to show that "distinctions on a racial basis . . . are odious and invidious."

Justice Frankfurter brought up what he called "certain facts of life," by which he referred to states "where there is a vast congregation of Negro population." He wanted Marshall to endorse gradual desegregation, but Marshall refused: If he did, Marshall said, he "would have to throw completely aside the personal and present rights" of his clients.

The South Carolina case produced the rhetorical high points of the arguments in the five segregation cases. Kansas offered only a halfhearted defense of segregation; the Topeka school board had already decided to abandon segregation, and the Supreme Court actually had to ask the state's attorney general whether the state was going to defend its statute at all. The state's case was presented by an assistant who had never argued a case in *any* appeals court, even in Kansas.

South Carolina was different. Governor Byrnes personally traveled to New York to hire a special lawyer to represent the state in the Supreme Court. John W. Davis, a native of West Virginia and deeply committed to maintaining segregation, was the country's most experienced Supreme Court advocate. Davis had been solicitor general under Woodrow Wilson, and had been the Democratic candidate for the presidency in 1924. In 1952 he was almost eighty, and was the leading partner in a major New York law firm. He agreed to donate his services to defending South Carolina, and segregation, in the Supreme Court.

Davis's oral argument was eloquent in an old-fashioned way. He gave the justices an effective description of the building program Byrnes had begun. When Justice Burton again asked about

John W. Davis, the lawyer who argued in
*Brown v. Board of Education* that school
segregation was constitutional

"changed conditions," Davis replied, "Changed conditions may affect policy, but changed conditions cannot broaden the terminology of the Constitution." He derided the psychological evidence about self-image as "fragmentary expertise based on an unexamined presupposition."

Davis began his closing argument by quoting W. E. B. Du Bois, who appeared to endorse segregation in some editorials he wrote in the 1930s: "We shall get a finer, better balance of spirit . . . by putting children in schools where they are wanted . . . than in thrusting them into hells where they are ridiculed and hated." Du Bois didn't exactly defend segregation, however; as he saw it in 1935 it was something inevitable, which the African-American community had to live with. For Davis, segregation ought to be left to the legislative process, where "those most immediately affected by it" could decide what to do.

Marshall responded to Davis in a matter-of-fact way. He stressed that "individual rights of minority people are not to be left to even the most mature judgment of the majority." Public opinion polls had nothing to do with constitutional interpretation. Marshall also tried to invoke the ideal of the rule of law by saying that he did not believe "that the people in South Carolina or those southern states are lawless people." If the Court said that segregation was unconstitutional, Marshall implied, the white South would go along.

Marshall ended his rebuttal with one of the most powerful images he ever offered the Court: "[I]n the South where I spent most of my time, you will see white and colored kids going down the road together to school. They separate and go to different schools, and they come out and play together. I do not see why there would necessarily be any trouble if they went to school together." The children,

Marshall showed the Court, played peacefully together, only to be separated at the school door by the force of law. That, he implied, was intolerable.

After hearing oral arguments the justices usually meet in what they call "the conference" to discuss the cases and take a preliminary vote on what to do. The justices realized that the segregation cases were probably the most important cases they would ever decide, and they also realized that they really didn't know what to do with them. Instead of voting, suggested Vinson, Jackson, and Frankfurter, the justices should simply bat around their ideas to see where things stood.

Fred Vinson, a stolid and unemotional man whom many outside the Court expected to vote against overruling *Plessy,* indicated how the cases were likely to turn out when he told his colleagues that "boldness is essential but wisdom indispensable" in dealing with the cases.[6] The "bold" course was obviously to strike segregation down; the "wise" one was to do it while endorsing gradualism. But, as Vinson made his rambling comments on the cases, he indicated that he was puzzled about how to deal with the Fourteenth Amendment's history.

Four justices came down firmly against segregation. Hugo Black said that he was "driven" to the conclusion that segregation was unconstitutional, even though he was convinced as well that "this means trouble," and that there "will be some violence" as desegregation took hold. Harold Burton referred with pride to his actions as mayor of Cleveland to desegregate the city's hospitals. William Douglas and Sherman Minton also said they would hold segregation unconstitutional.

[6]Quoted from Hutchinson, "Unanimity and Desegregation," p. 91.

Supreme Court Justice Minton

Justice Stanley Reed, a Kentuckian appointed to the Court in 1938, was the only one to say that the states should be allowed to "work out the problems for themselves." Tom Clark said that he would agree with Reed if a majority insisted on immediate desegregation, but he would "go along" with a decision requiring gradual desegregation.

Felix Frankfurter and Robert Jackson held the keys to getting the Court to act. Everyone on the Court agreed that it would be terrible for the Court to strike down segregation by a narrow margin, and most wanted the decision to be unanimous. Unfortunately, Jackson and Frankfurter each had problems with the legal theories Marshall had put forth.

Jackson's were the most serious. Widely regarded as a "lawyer's lawyer," Jackson had grown up in upstate New York, and, as he put it, he was "not conscious of the problem" of segregation until he came to Washington with the Roosevelt administration. He was bothered by the "conscious or unconscious emotional commitments of one sort or another" on both sides of the issue, and wanted to work out a "wise" solution to the problem. For Jackson, wisdom meant that, although he had "no sympathy with racial conceits which underlie segregation policies," the Court had to take "widely held beliefs and attitudes" into account, as part of good "law and statecraft."

Jackson rapidly decided that getting rid of segregation was good policy. He never quite convinced himself that it was good *law*. One of his law clerks at the time, William H. Rehnquist—later to be appointed to the Supreme Court by Richard Nixon and made Chief Justice by Ronald Reagan—wrote a memorandum saying that *Plessy* "was right and should be re-affirmed." The case against segrega-

William H. Rehnquist (appointed by President Nixon to the Supreme Court) wrote, as law clerk to Jackson, that *Plessy v. Ferguson* should not be overturned.

tion, Rehnquist wrote, was "sociological" and not constitutional. Constitutional law, Rehnquist told Jackson, couldn't rest on "the personal predilections of the Justices," but Marshall's effort to "convince the Court of the moral wrongness" of segregation asked them to enact their personal policy views into law. That, Rehnquist said, would never work.

Jackson was more ambivalent about what he ought to do than Rehnquist's memo indicated. During the conference discussion of the cases, Jackson made the forceful statement that "Marshall's brief starts [and] ends with sociology," and he said that he thought that "it will be bad for the [N]egroes to be put into white schools." But, he continued, although he wouldn't accept immediate desegregation, he would "go along" with a ruling allowing time for desegregation.

Felix Frankfurter also was troubled by the cases. A bubbly man who incessantly lobbied his colleagues—and regularly annoyed them with his efforts to get them to see things his way—Frankfurter thought of himself as the Court's scholar, devoted in an almost religious way to "the law" and opposed to those who treated constitutional law simply as politics. At the same time, Frankfurter thought of himself as a person closely attuned to American politics. He suggested delaying a decision until a new administration took office, because "the social gains of having [desegregation] accomplished with executive action would be enormous." He believed that his lawyer friends in the South could become the focus of moderate efforts to implement desegregation, if only the justices demonstrated enough sympathy for the burdens desegregation placed on the white South.

The tension between law and politics almost

immobilized Frankfurter in the segregation cases. Because he couldn't quite figure out what to do, he was particularly irritated at the self-confidence Black and Douglas displayed in their comments opposing segregation. Jackson was saying that getting rid of segregation was good policy, and Frankfurter agreed. Jackson was also saying, however, that there was no good legal argument against segregation. Jackson was willing to "go along" despite that. Frankfurter was not. Disdainful of those who treated law as politics, Frankfurter needed to develop a *legal* theory against segregation.

By the time the justices' initial discussion ended, no one knew where the Court as a whole was. Probably, if they had been forced to decide whether to insist on immediate desegregation, the justices would have voted "no" by a substantial margin. If they had been forced to decide between gradual desegregation and continued segregation, the justices would have found segregation unconstitutional, with a dissent likely from Reed.

No one, however, was pushing the justices to decide. Vinson as chief justice had some power to move things along if he wanted to, but he was not a forceful leader. The four justices committed to striking segregation down wanted a nearly unanimous vote, and they were willing to bide their time if that would help. Jackson was so lukewarm about striking segregation down that he wasn't likely to lead, and Frankfurter was so torn by his concerns about law and politics that he couldn't.

The possibility of delaying a decision had come up several times during the conference discussion. The reasons for delay varied: to get the views of a new administration, to get more discussion of how to justify gradual desegregation in light of the principle that constitutional rights were "personal and present," and to work out some more technical problems. In June, almost six months after the cases had been argued, the Court ordered the parties to come back again in the fall and reargue the cases. Frankfurter drafted five questions they should address in particular. Two asked about the intentions of the Fourteenth Amendment's framers, and one asked about judicial power to order desegregation if the framers' intentions were unclear. The other two asked whether a court could order gradual desegregation, and if so, exactly what form an order directing gradual desegregation should take.

# Chapter 5
# THE WARREN COURT

John W. Davis told the Court at the reargument, "I suppose there are few invitations less welcome in an advocate's life than to be asked to reargue a case on which he has once spent himself." The invitation was even less welcome to Marshall. The very fact that the Court ordered reargument indicated that it was divided. The earlier university cases had been decided quickly and unanimously. What, Marshall wondered, made the current segregation cases so much harder for the justices? Only that the social consequences of a decision in his clients' favor would be so much more far-reaching. But, as an advocate, Marshall could hardly say much to allay the justices' concerns about that.

The precise questions the Court asked were also troubling. Marshall had said all he could on the question of remedy. His reargument would go over familiar ground, which hardly made the prospect of reargument attractive. The historical questions were even more difficult. From research in the university cases Marshall knew that the historical material seemed to undermine his position. Marshall's strength as an oral advocate was in laying out the compelling moral case against segregation; he found it hard to work the details of legislative history into an equally compelling oral argument.

During the summer before the reargument Marshall assembled a team of volunteer historians and lawyers to look into the specific history behind the Fourteenth Amendment and the more general intellectual and political currents that influenced the amendment's framers. What turned up about the specific history was quite discouraging. There was basically nothing showing that the framers wanted to prohibit or get rid of segregated schools, a lot showing that the framers weren't terribly troubled by the possibility that schools would be segregated, and not much showing that they hoped the courts would eventually say that segregation was barred by the Fourteenth Amendment.

The more general history was much more helpful. The framers' humanitarianism argued against the view that they would have approved segregated schools in the world as it had come to be in the 1950s: Schools were more important than they had been, and segregation was a component of a more virulent system treating African-Americans as second-class citizens than they might have expected it to be.

Shortly before the reargument Marshall called his team together for a conference to thrash out what to do. The aim was to figure out how to "neutralize" the troubling historical material, for, as Marshall put it, a "nothin' to nothin' score means we win the ball game." Historians Alfred Kelly and

John Hope Franklin worked closely with Bob Ming, an African-American law professor at the University of Chicago, and staff lawyers to hammer out a solution. At first they tried to avoid the details of what the framers thought about school segregation itself, but Marshall told them that would "never get past Frankfurter."[7]

Their second try was more successful. The trick was to give the justices a setting into which they could place the framers' views about segregation. That setting, the NAACP lawyers argued, was strongly egalitarian. Over the course of their long struggle against slavery, the framers had developed the view that racial differences were entirely irrelevant to social life. True, as a matter of political expediency they sometimes had to compromise their views, as Congress did in authorizing segregated schools in the District of Columbia. But, the lawyers argued, when the framers came to the task of revising the Constitution, they meant to embed their egalitarian principles in our fundamental law. If political circumstances meant that they could not *enact* full equality in the late 1860s, still they wanted to ensure that the nation was committed to principles of equality that *could* be enacted when circumstances changed. It went without saying that in our constitutional system judges exercising the power of judicial review were the ones to decide whether circumstances had changed.

That argument got Marshall over the hurdle of the adverse historical material. He still had to

---

[7]Alfred Kelly, "An Inside View of 'Brown v. Board,'" delivered to the American Historical Association, December 1961, reprinted in Senate Judiciary Committee, 87th Congress, 1st Session, Hearings on the Nomination of Thurgood Marshall, quoted in Mark Tushnet, *Making Civil Rights Law: Thurgood Marshall and the Supreme Court, 1935–1961* (New York: Oxford University Press, 1994), pp. 196, 198, 199.

worry about the Court's questions about appropri-
ate remedy. Jack Greenberg and David Pinsky, two
young white lawyers on Marshall's staff, grappled
with the problem. Clearly the Court was interested
in some gradual remedy, perhaps resting on the
theory that courts were allowed to "balance" competing considerations, including the possibility of
resistance, in developing a remedy. Could that be
reconciled with the principle that constitutional
rights were "personal and present"? Even more, as
a lawyer representing individual clients, could
Marshall responsibly argue for some gradual remedy that might not give his individual clients anything at all?

Greenberg and Pinsky worked out the answer
that Marshall gave the Court. Balancing competing
considerations was barely acceptable where constitutional rights were involved. But, because balancing was questionable from the outset, the courts
should take only a limited range of matters into
account. Of course, school boards had to be given
time to adjust their student assignment policies.
For example, if they moved from a segregated system to a neighborhood school system, they had to
be given some time to draw the boundaries. The
courts should not consider, however, anything
other than these administrative matters, and they
should decisively reject the proposition that the
possibility of resistance justified delay. As Marshall
put it in his homely way, "I am for the gradual
approach, [but] 91 years since the Emancipation
Proclamation has been gradual enough."

Gradualism preoccupied the Justice Department. President Truman's department had supported the NAACP in the first argument. A new administration was in place, though, and its political concerns differed from Truman's. Instead of seeing
African-Americans in the North as part of a Demo-

President Dwight D. Eisenhower appointed Earl Warren
chief justice of the Supreme Court.

cratic coalition, President Dwight D. Eisenhower's administration thought that it could make inroads on Democratic support in the South. Endorsing the NAACP's attack on segregation would hardly help. Eisenhower himself was at best lukewarm about desegregation. The administration's policy in the segregation cases was set by Eisenhower's attorney general, Herbert Brownell. Brownell came from the Republican party's Northern wing, which saw the party as the "party of Lincoln" and was still deeply committed to civil rights.

There was a leadership vacuum in the Justice Department when the time came to develop a position in the segregation cases. Neither Brownell nor his assistant on civil rights issues could devote much time to the question. That left matters in the hands of career lawyers in the office of the solicitor general. There Philip Elman took charge. Elman was a protégé of Felix Frankfurter, with whom—in a rather striking breach of judicial ethics—he discussed the cases as he developed the government's position. Elman therefore knew that Frankfurter desperately needed some justification for allowing gradual desegregation.

Elman had drafted the government's brief in the first argument, which made what Elman later called the "entirely unprincipled" argument that desegregation could occur gradually. He had not spelled out the argument in detail. For the reargument, Elman did a little more. Desegregation decrees could take "administrative obstacles" into account; these included transportation questions and teacher transfers. Elman's brief finessed the hard question of white opposition with the optimistic statement that experiences with desegregation in the armed forces showed that it could occur "without disorder or friction."

The government's position actually tracked the NAACP's quite closely. Elman told the Court that the government's analysis of history was "an objective non-adversary discussion." Then it described the general background of equal rights before turning to the specifics of the Fourteenth Amendment. This was exactly the structure of the NAACP's approach. Coming from the government and presented as "objective," it surely was a strong endorsement of the NAACP position.

Two events made the reargument largely irrelevant to the outcome in the segregation cases. One occurred inside the Court. Justice Frankfurter was in many ways the chief obstacle to a decision, because at first he did not know how to reconcile the outcome he desired with what he believed the law required. During the summer before the scheduled reargument, Frankfurter had his law clerk go through the history of the Fourteenth Amendment's framing for himself. Even before Frankfurter read the competing briefs the Court had asked for, he had the law clerk's research in hand.

Unlike the NAACP and the United States, Frankfurter's clerk concentrated on the details of the framing. His conclusion was that Congress really had not focused much attention on what they meant to do in proposing the amendment. "A blunderbuss was simply aimed in the direction of existing evils in the South," he wrote, and "it was preposterous to worry about unsegregated schools . . . when hardly a beginning had been made at educating Negroes at all."[8] This research was

---

[8]Alexander Bickel to Felix Frankfurter, Aug. 22, 1953, *Felix Frankfurter Papers,* Reel 71, file 15, Harvard Law School, quoted in Tushnet, *Making Civil Rights Law,* p. 203.

enough for Frankfurter. In circulating it to the other justices, Frankfurter told them that it showed that the history was "inconclusive": Congress didn't outlaw segregation, but it didn't endorse segregation either.

With this research completed, Frankfurter was ready to move. Yet, it is not clear that the research should have satisfied Frankfurter. If Congress in the Fourteenth Amendment did not "manifest" an intention to outlaw segregation, as Frankfurter agreed, where did the Court get its authority to outlaw it? Probably the research was important to Frankfurter less for what it showed than for the fact that it allowed Frankfurter to see himself as having made an important contribution to the Court's deliberations. He had derided Justice Black's confident reliance on the "basic purpose" of the Fourteenth Amendment; he was barely on speaking terms with Douglas; and he could scarcely conceal his contempt for justices he called the "great libertarians," whom he thought would have landed the Court "in the soup" if they had their way. Somehow Frankfurter had to assure himself that no one, including himself, would attribute a decision against segregation primarily to the "great libertarians." The law clerk's research allowed Frankfurter to explain to himself and others how crucial Frankfurter's role in the decision was.

Frankfurter would not have been an obstacle to decision, however, if someone else had taken a firm hand in leading the Court. Chief Justice Fred Vinson was not the person to do that. On September 8, 1952, Vinson died of a heart attack. Earl Warren, Vinson's successor, *would* lead the Court to a decision.

As a politician in California, Warren had supported the internment of Japanese Americans

Chief Justice Earl Warren

upheld in *Korematsu*. He became a progressive Republican governor of California, and was the Republican vice-presidential candidate in 1948. At a key moment during the 1952 party convention Warren directed California's delegates to vote in favor of a motion that effectively gave the nomination to Eisenhower over his chief rival Robert A. Taft. Indebted to Warren, Eisenhower promised to nominate Warren for the first Supreme Court vacancy during his presidential term. Eisenhower had not expected the vacancy to be the chief justice's position, but, after only a short hesitation, he nominated Warren for the position.

Warren had no qualms about finding segregation unconstitutional. He was not a deep constitutional theorist, but segregation was so wrong that it *had* to be unconstitutional. Perhaps more important, Warren was a vigorous and talented manager. He was open and gregarious, always willing to sit down and talk about sports—or anything else— with his colleagues. They in turn were willing to let him take the lead in hard cases.

Warren's appointment meant that the Court was sure to find segregation unconstitutional. The law clerk's research meant that Frankfurter was ready to climb on board. The only question was whether the Court's decision would be unanimous. Unfortunately, a tedious set of rearguments still had to take place before the Court actually got down to deciding the cases.

Once again John W. Davis gave the Court an oral argument, the last of his career. Without interruption, Davis took on the argument that the abolitionist background of the Fourteenth Amendment's framers showed that they were egalitarians; actually, Davis said, all they wanted was to abolish slavery, not establish social equality. He concluded his statement—more a speech than an oral argument—by saying, "Somewhere, sometime to every principle comes a moment of repose when it has been so often announced, so confidently relied upon, so long continued, that it passes the limits of judicial discretion and disturbance." Would desegregating the schools in South Carolina "make the children any happier," Davis asked. "Would they learn any more quickly? Would their lives be more serene?" He evoked a past era of political rhetoric in saying, "Here is equal education, not promised, not prophesied, but present. Shall it be thrown away on some fancied question of racial prestige?"

Davis implicitly referred to white fears of desegregation. Virginia's lawyer was somewhat more direct. Pointing out that there were about equal numbers of African-American and white students in Barbara Johns's school district, the lawyer asked incredulously, "Shall we put one Negro along with every white child in high school when that is the best high school?"

Although Marshall's initial argument had been diffuse, his opponents energized him. He disparaged their references to what he called the "horrible number of Negroes in the South." He took on Davis's reference to prestige by saying, "I understand them to say that it is just a little feeling on the part of Negroes." Davis was "exactly right. Ever since the Emancipation Proclamation, the Negro has been trying to get . . . the same status as anybody else regardless of race." At the end of his rebuttal, Marshall returned to the image of African-American and white children playing before and after school. There was, Marshall said, "some magic to it." The Supreme Court's cases established that the children could live in the same neighborhoods, but segregationists believed that "if they go to elementary and high school the world will fall apart." The only defense of that position, Marshall concluded, "is to find that for some reason Negroes are inferior to all other human beings." But "nobody will stand in the Court and urge that." It was time, he said, "that this Court should make it clear that that is not what our Constitution stands for."

The rearguments did little to clarify matters, but with Warren ready to push the cases along that hardly mattered. The justices discussed the case at their conference on December 12, 1953, and it was clear that a majority was now ready to invalidate segregation. Warren said that he rejected *Plessy's* premise of Negro inferiority, and did not "see how segregation can be justified in this day and age." The Court's decision, Warren said, should invalidate segregation "in a tolerant way," expressing understanding for the different "condition[s] in the different states." Warren thought that it would "take all the wisdom of this Court to dispose of the matter with a minimum of emotion and strife." Although several other justices hoped that ending segregation would not, as Warren put it, "cause trouble," Justice Clark cautioned that "violence will follow in the south." Still, he said, he didn't "like the system of segregation and [would] vote to abolish it," but he wanted the remedy to be "carefully worked out."

Justice Jackson continued to assert that "this is a political question." He still was not sure that Marshall had offered "a judicial basis for a congenial political conclusion." But, he said, "as a political decision, I can go along with" overturning segregation. Later he drafted an opinion, never published, expressing sympathy for the claims of the white South, who were being "coerced" out of segregation. "[T]he Northern majority of this Court," Jackson wrote, should not be "self-righteous." He disagreed, too, with the premise that the Court must act "because our representative system has failed." But, Jackson wrote, he would invalidate segregation because it rested on a "factual assumption," that the races were quite different, that time and experience had proven false. People had to be evaluated "as individuals and not as a race for their learning, aptitude and discipline," particularly because of the importance of education in the modern world. "Present-day conditions," for Jackson, meant that the Court had to "strike from our books the doctrine of separate-but-equal facilities."

Jackson had a serious heart attack in March, and Warren regularly went to the hospital to keep him up to date on the Court's work, and to persuade him not to publish a separate opinion in the segregation cases. Only Stanley Reed had said that he wouldn't vote to overrule *Plessy*, and Warren went to work on him too. Warren appealed to Reed not to dissent alone. A dissenting opinion, Warren believed, could only give white Southerners ammunition in what many expected to be a difficult effort to implement the Court's decision, however much they hoped that the white South would comply. In the end Reed agreed to swallow his disagreements and join the rest of the Court.

Warren insisted that the opinion be easy to read and understand. Although the South Carolina case had gotten to the Supreme Court first, the decision was handed down under the name of *Brown v. Board of Education*. Brown's case got a lower number on the Court's list after the Court sent the South Carolina one back to Judge Parker's

The Supreme Court of 1954, which ruled in the
*Brown v. Board of Education* case

court to get its views on South Carolina's progress toward equalization.

The opinion Warren and his law clerks wrote was only a few pages long. It was issued on May 17, 1954. After describing the background of the cases the Court was considering, Warren's opinion called the historical material "inconclusive." Strong supporters of the Fourteenth Amendment "undoubtedly intended them to remove all legal distinctions" among people, while "[t]heir opponents, just as certainly, were antagonistic to both the letter and the spirit of the Amendments and wished them to have the most limited effect. What others . . . had in mind cannot be determined with any degree of certainty."

Part of the problem, Warren wrote, was "the status of public education" in 1868. Public education in the South was at a rudimentary stage, and even in the North public education was completely unlike public education in 1954. This led Warren to conclude that, in deciding the cases, "we cannot turn the clock back to 1868 when the [Fourteenth] Amendment was adopted, or even to 1896 when *Plessy v. Ferguson* was written." The Court "must consider public education in light of its full development and its present place in American life throughout the nation." Seen in that light, "education is perhaps the most important function of state and local governments." It "is the very foundation of good citizenship. Today it is a principal instrument in awakening the child to cultural values, in preparing him for later professional training, and in helping him to adjust normally to his environment."

Segregation, Warren said, deprived children of equal educational opportunities. "To separate them from others of similar age and qualifications solely

Thurgood Marshall (left) and two NAACP lawyers
who worked on *Brown v. Board of Education,*
James Nabrit (center) and Jack Greenberg (right)

because of their race generates a feeling of inferiority as to their status in the community that may affect their hearts and minds in a way unlikely ever to be undone." Warren quoted the trial court's finding in the Kansas case, that segregation had a detrimental effect on African-American children. In a footnote Warren pointed to "modern authority," including the Clarks' doll study, giving support to that finding.

Warren's discussion of the issue took only eight paragraphs. It ended, "We conclude that in the field of public education the doctrine of 'separate but equal' has no place. Separate educational facilities are inherently unequal."

That did not end the opinion, however. The question of remedy remained. The Court did not decide it, though. Instead it asked for a third argument, this one limited to the question of remedy. A year later, after the third argument, the Court issued its decision in *Brown v. Board of Education II*, requiring school systems to desegregate with "all deliberate speed." That phrase set the slow pace of desegregation for a decade.

Everyone involved in the lawsuits—lawyers and justices alike—found it hard to talk candidly about the issue of remedy. Everyone knew that, as a technical or administrative matter, it wouldn't be hard to eliminate segregation. All a school board had to do in assigning children to schools was adopt some method that didn't rely on race: a neighborhood school system, or admission to particular schools on the basis of test results. As Marshall put it in the third argument, "They give tests to grade children so what do we think is the solution? Simple. Put the dumb colored children in with the dumb white children, and put the smart colored children with the smart white children." Putting such a nonracial system in place might take a little time, but not much. Whenever Marshall or the United States' lawyers had to come up with a time for *that* sort of compliance, they never estimated more than a year.

Unhappily, everyone also knew that these administrative problems weren't the real ones. The fear was that the white South would resist the Court's directive to eliminate segregation, perhaps with violence as Justice Clark had said. During the third set of arguments, lawyers for South Carolina and Virginia straightforwardly said that they could not assure the Court that the people of their states would "conform" to a decree directing that white and African-American children attend the same schools "in the reasonably foreseeable future." Marshall's response was to express "shock" at these observations, and said genially, "Sure, there will be noise here and there, but we have got to continue."

Even Marshall knew that there would be more than noise. Before the third round of arguments he had his staff investigate conditions in several Southern states. In border areas, desegregation had already begun; indeed, in February 1955 the Topeka school board voted to complete desegregation by adopting a full neighborhood school policy. Elsewhere, though, the staff expected resistance, and anticipated some reluctance from within the African-American community to efforts that would place schoolchildren at risk of violent reactions.

What, though, could be done? Marshall's ethical duties to his clients meant that he had to insist on a decree that would require desegregation immediately, or "forthwith," as the lawyers put it. There was more to Marshall's position than a judgment about legal ethics, however. What, after all, did "immediate" desegregation really mean? Marshall knew that, as a practical matter, it was going to take time, not to redraw school district boundaries, but to persuade African-American parents to put their children in a new school setting. He also knew that white Southerners were going to resist any efforts to desegregate. So, in practical terms, "immediate" desegregation really meant that the courts would order school boards to admit a handful of African-American children to previously white schools, and otherwise the schools would remain racially separate for at least a few years. "Immediate" desegregation, as Marshall understood it, really was "delayed" desegregation.

On the Supreme Court, Justice Hugo Black shared Marshall's understanding. Black, joined by William O. Douglas, pressed his colleagues to require desegregation "forthwith," although Black too knew that this would not mean immediate desegregation. Black had a different concern. He knew that the white South would resist desegregation. For Black the question was, what Supreme Court decision was most consistent with the ideal of the rule of law? The answer was simple: Constitutional rights were personal and present, and the Court should say so. The lower courts would preserve the ideal of the rule of law by directing the admission of the few African-American students who wanted to go to desegregated schools under stressful circumstances. If whites resisted those orders, the rest of the country—and the world—would see that they rejected the rule of law. A gradualist remedy, allowing the white South time to adjust to the new constitutional rule announced in *Brown,* would give whites "cover" for their resistance. Instead of rejecting the Court's requirements, they would be able to say

Supreme Court justice William O. Douglas,
a consistent liberal on the Court

that they were doing their best to comply, but—as the gradualist remedy allowed—they had to take their time about it.

Although their insistence on "immediate" desegregation seemed to take an optimistic view of what the courts could accomplish, Black and Douglas were actually quite pessimistic. They strongly believed that the Court had to announce the fundamental principle that segregation was unconstitutional, but they had no illusions about getting the South to go along.

Advocates of gradualism, like Frankfurter, were far more optimistic. By displaying sensitivity to the concerns of the white South, the gradualists believed, the Court could persuade the white South to go along with desegregation.

The gradualists were also scared away by the picture the word "immediate" conveyed. When Marshall asked for "immediate" desegregation, the gradualists thought that he really had in mind equal numbers of African-American and white children attending the same schools within a year. Of course the *word* did suggest that, but Marshall, Black, and Douglas knew enough about social reality to understand that the world would not dramatically change if the Supreme Court issued a decision saying that desegregation had to occur "forthwith."

There was, however, no real *debate* between those seeking immediate desegregation and the gradualists. The Court had reached a unanimous decision to invalidate segregation only because most of the justices thought that such a decision went hand in glove with a gradualist remedy. The only real question was how to explain why gradualism was consistent with the tradition that treated constitutional rights as personal and present.

The justices fumbled around for a solution. Should they say that the lower courts should direct school boards to admit only "named plaintiffs" like Barbara Johns and Linda Brown to desegregated schools? Or should they treat the cases as "class actions" and tell lower courts to order school boards to admit all African-American children to desegregated schools? Should they figure out a timetable for desegregation themselves, or should they let lower courts develop timetables for each district? Should they say anything about what really worried them, the possibility of white resistance, or should they write an opinion that talked only about the administrative problems of achieving desegregation?

None of the alternatives was entirely satisfactory. If overruling *Plessy* meant anything, it meant that school boards couldn't take race into account in assigning students to schools. Yet, how could a court say to a school board, "You can't take race into account in assigning Linda Brown to a school, because she filed a lawsuit, but you can take it into account when assigning every other child in the district to a school"? If the Court sent the cases to lower courts to set timetables, desegregation might take a long time in places where even the federal judges might be uncomfortable with the Court's ruling. Yet, how could the Supreme Court, sitting in Washington, tell school boards in Wilmington, Delaware; Atlanta, Georgia; and rural Virginia how quickly they could put a desegregation plan into effect?

Again Chief Justice Warren wrote the opinion, handed down on May 31, 1955, and again it was quite short. This time, though, Warren did not try to make the opinion "educational," as Frankfurter had urged. It simply tried to get the cases out of the Supreme Court's hands. Warren stressed that "school authorities have the primary responsibility" for solving the "varied local problems" that might arise during desegregation. The lower courts would then decide whether the school boards were trying to desegregate in "good faith." In working out desegregation orders, Warren told lower courts, they should use "practical flexibility" in "adjusting and reconciling public and private needs." On one side were the "personal interest[s] of the plaintiffs in admission to public schools as soon as practicable on a nondiscriminatory basis." Accomplishing that, however, meant overcoming "a variety of obstacles" that the lower courts could take into account. But, Warren wrote, "It should go without saying that the vitality of these constitutional principles cannot be allowed to yield simply because of disagreement with them."

After this indirect reference to the possibility of white resistance, Warren returned to a more optimistic vision of what ought to happen. He directed lower courts to try to ensure that school boards made "a prompt and reasonable start toward full compliance" with *Brown*. Once they started, the boards might discover new problems—with "the physical condition of the school plant, the school transportation system, personnel, revision of school districts and attendance areas" into neighborhood school zones—and might ask for more time, but the boards had to show that the problems were real and that delays were consistent with "good faith compliance at the earliest practicable date."

Warren summarized the remedy with a phrase that became notorious: The lower courts should enter whatever orders were "necessary and proper to admit to public schools on a racially nondiscriminatory basis *with all deliberate speed* the parties to these cases." Warren picked up the "all deliberate speed" phrase from Frankfurter and the United States' brief written by Philip Elman. It came from a 1911 case dealing with how Virginia and West Virginia should pay off debts incurred before West Virginia broke away from Virginia during the Civil War.

The "all deliberate speed" phrase showed how hard the Court thought the problem of desegregation was. "Deliberation" suggested thoughtfulness and a rather stately pace, while "speed" suggested a more rapid process. The administrative problems Warren's opinion mentioned were hardly enough to make it difficult for a school board to delay desegregation for more than a year. Warren's opinion gave the game away when it said what "should go without saying." No one really believed the administrative problems were serious. What was going to make desegregation difficult was "disagreement" with *Brown's* constitutional principles. Frankfurter believed that leading Southern white lawyers, committed to the rule of law, could—if the Court gave them time—bring the rest of the white South along. He was wrong.

# Chapter 6

# WITH ALL DELIBERATE SPEED

Border states began to comply with *Brown* rather quickly. Some districts adopted neighborhood school plans, and others allowed children to attend whatever school they wanted as long as the school had space available. These programs did eliminate race as the basis for student assignment, but often they did little to make schools biracial. St. Louis adopted a neighborhood school plan, for example, but because of severe residential segregation only a few African-American children attended schools with a majority of whites.

Marshall and the NAACP staff accepted these plans, because they believed the school boards were indeed complying with *Brown* in good faith. Even more, in 1955 the NAACP lawyers would have accepted all sorts of plans that later they rejected: plans calling for desegregating high schools first, then junior highs, then elementary

schools, or plans that would have extended desegregation over a twelve-year period, as schools
desegregated one grade level a year.

Why did Marshall and his colleagues accept
neighborhood school and freedom-of-choice systems
that still separated children of different races? In
part, of course, they had to. Getting the white
South to do anything at all was a major accom-
plishment. What later was called "token" integration was a large step in 1955 and 1956. Perhaps,
Marshall thought, the South would do more as
time went on.

In part, though, they accepted token integration because the principle *Brown* stood for was less
clear than it came to seem. When the lower court
in South Carolina reconsidered the Summerton
case, Judge Parker took one view. *Brown,* he wrote,
"does not require integration. It merely forbids discrimination . . . the use of governmental power to
enforce segregation." Accordingly, as long as school
boards used some reason *other than race* to assign
children to schools, they were complying with
*Brown.* Directing children to attend the school
nearest their homes, for example, didn't rely on
race. On this view, even if neighborhoods were so
segregated that no integration occurred, a neighborhood school policy was enough to satisfy *Brown.*

Parker's interpretation of *Brown* found some
support in the Court's language. In referring to the
harms segregation caused, *Brown* had indeed spoken of separation "solely because of . . . race."
Marshall's legal strategy, too, had repeatedly
emphasized that the fundamental principle at
stake was that governments could not use race to
justify any of their decisions. As long as governments took race out of the picture, the basic principle was satisfied no matter what the actual results:

To use Marshall's example of testing children for school admission, if there were lots of dumb white kids and few dumb African-American kids in a district, the tests might produce classrooms that were largely one-race, but that was all right. There was a competing interpretation of *Brown*, though, which had been only slightly below the surface as the justices considered the case. According to this interpretation, the Constitution aimed at substantial integration: making sure that children were in schools that had substantial numbers from every race in the school district. If segregated education generated feelings of inferiority "in a way unlikely ever to be undone," it did so largely because the races were separated in fact, not because they were separated by force of law. If children were harmed by segregated education because they did not have the opportunity to learn from social contacts with children of other races, they were harmed no matter what the *reason* for the racial separation. And, of course, unless integration was the outcome, why would anyone think that "desegregating" schools would be difficult? Getting boards to come up with some principle other than race as a way of assigning children to schools should have been simple. Desegregating schools would be hard, even in the face of white resistance, only if the ultimate goal was integration, not desegregation.

Uncertainty over what *Brown* meant, and the delay that the "all deliberate speed" formulation clearly authorized, gave the white South a chance to organize to resist *Brown*.

Most Southern Senators and many members of Congress endorsed the "Southern Manifesto" issued in 1956. The Manifesto called *Brown* an "unwarranted" abuse of judicial power, expressing the justices' "personal, political and social ideas" rather than constitutional law. The Manifesto's signers said that they would "use all lawful means" to reverse *Brown*. As powerful members of Congress, for example, some of the signers pushed the Internal Revenue Service to investigate the tax-exempt status of the NAACP's legal arm.

White Southerners also revived theories of states' rights that most people had thought discredited. A series of editorials in the Richmond, Virginia, *News Leader,* written by James Jackson Kilpatrick, restated a theory called "interposition" that, in a different form, had been defended by James Madison and Thomas Jefferson in the late 1790s. According to Kilpatrick's version of interposition, the Constitution allowed the states to "interpose" themselves between the national government, including the Supreme Court, and their citizens. If the national government issued orders that the states found inconsistent with the Constitution, the states could formally declare that they would not go along.

Future Supreme Court justice Lewis Powell debated Kilpatrick at a private Richmond club, and called Kilpatrick's theory nonsense. Powell, a respected lawyer and member of the city's school board, was unwilling to take his disagreement to the public, though, and Kilpatrick's editorials at least gave a facade of legal support for white resistance to *Brown*.

Elsewhere in the South ambitious politicians saw that they could use *Brown* as a focus for their political campaigns. In Arkansas, segregationists attacked governor Orval Faubus for failing to take a strong enough stand against desegregation. Faubus had previously been a relative moderate on race relations issues, but he feared for his political career and supported laws designed to make desegregation impossible.

Rural voters were more deeply committed to segregation than urban voters. This was at least in part because in the cities residential segregation meant that some forms of desegregation wouldn't actually lead to integration, while in rural areas, *anything* that eliminated race as a basis for student assignments would probably mean substantial integration. In Virginia, residents in the state's north, the suburbs of Washington, D.C., were much less concerned about maintaining segregation than were the white residents of Prince Edward County. Segregationists from rural areas were generally quite powerful in state legislatures, because of their seniority and because rural areas throughout the South had more seats in the legislature than their population justified. (The Supreme Court did not begin to require districts to satisfy the "one person, one vote" rule until the 1960s.)

Southern politicians developed three basic forms of opposition to *Brown*. The first might be called "passive" resistance—appearing to comply with *Brown* while actually doing nothing at all. The second was called "massive resistance"—flatly refusing to comply with *Brown* and forcing African-Americans and the federal courts to fight for every minor step toward eliminating segregation. The third was violent resistance.

North Carolina mastered the techniques of passive resistance. Its legislature adopted a statute directing school boards to assign students to schools by taking into account a long list of factors, including "orderly and efficient administration" and the "health, safety, and general welfare" of the students. A student who wanted to go to a school different from the one he or she attended the year before had to submit a detailed application form and have a personal interview. Then, if the application was denied, the student had to appeal to the school board and ultimately to a court.

Notably, the North Carolina statute did not refer to race at all, so it seemed to comply with Judge Parker's interpretation of *Brown*. Of course, what really mattered was how school boards applied the statute. And, of course, they regularly applied it to discriminate against African-American students who sought to enroll in the white schools.

Technically, *applying* in a discriminatory way a statute that didn't refer to race was just as great a constitutional violation as enacting a statute that *did* refer to race. The Supreme Court had said so in *Yick Wo v. Hopkins,* decided in 1886. San Francisco had an ordinance that banned laundries in wooden buildings, unless the city's board of supervisors approved. A Chinese laundry owner challenged the ordinance, not on the ground that it was unreasonable (laundries in wooden buildings did indeed pose a greater risk of fire than laundries in brick buildings), but because the board of supervisors administered the process to discriminate: Over 200 Chinese laundry operators tried to get a permit to operate in wooden buildings, and all had been denied, while the board had granted permission to all but one white applicant.

In the long run North Carolina couldn't get away with its passive resistance. In the short run, though, very few African-American children attended schools with whites in North Carolina. The Supreme Court had a chance to speed things up in 1958, when NAACP lawyer Robert Carter asked it to say that students didn't have to appeal denials of their applications, but the Court, afraid of getting even more involved in the desegregation process, didn't intervene.

Virginia pioneered massive resistance, adopting statutes that legislatures elsewhere in the South took as models. Massive resistance involved a package of laws aimed at preventing desegregation. One statute created a statewide board to assign students to schools. Another authorized the state government to take over the operation of any local school district where desegregation was about to occur, either by voluntary choice of the school board or by order of a federal court. The governor was supposed to investigate and return the district to local control if "the peace and tranquility of the community" would not be disturbed. Otherwise the state would run the schools on a segregated basis— or close them. The state also planned to give parents grants to pay tuition at private schools if all else failed, but the state supreme court said that the state constitution didn't permit that.

As a *legal* strategy for avoiding desegregation, massive resistance was a failure: The federal courts invalidated all the important parts of the program. Doing so took a lot of time and energy, however, which made massive resistance a *practical* success. As in North Carolina, only a handful of African-American students attended desegregated schools by the end of the 1950s. The Prince Edward County schools shut down for five years, as whites refused to go along with the inevitable desegregation orders.

One reason challenging massive resistance was difficult was that the package had another component: an attack on the NAACP and its lawyers. So, instead of spending time challenging segregation, the organization had to spend time defending itself. Virginia charged the NAACP's lawyers with an old-fashioned ethical violation called *barratry,* which basically meant that the NAACP's lawyers brought lawsuits not because clients wanted to sue but because the *lawyers* wanted to sue. That wasn't true; the NAACP's lawyers always had real clients who really wanted to eliminate segregation. Still, there was enough evidence of activities resembling barratry—speeches by lawyers urging people to come forward to sue, for example—that fighting the charge was difficult.

Other states tried to shut the NAACP down by saying it hadn't obtained a license or paid the taxes out-of-state corporations had to pay. The NAACP was perfectly willing to pay the taxes or get the licenses, but that wasn't the point of the states' actions. The states wanted to use these licensing proceedings to get lists of local NAACP members. Then, whites in the community could harass or terrorize NAACP members, effectively driving it out of the state.

Eventually the Supreme Court struck down all these tactics, finding that the NAACP and its lawyers were protected by the free speech provisions of the Constitution. Membership lists could be kept secret precisely because a government demand exposed members to serious trouble. Yet, once again, these tactics preoccupied the NAACP, making it even more difficult to focus on the desegregation process. Alabama managed to shut the NAACP down for almost eight years, which meant that no one was in a position to bring a lawsuit trying to desegregate any Alabama schools for that whole period.

If all else failed to stop desegregation, violence might succeed—or so some white Southerners thought. The Little Rock school crisis of 1957–58 proved them wrong. It did demonstrate the lengths to which resistance would go in combating the rule of law with the rule of force. But it also showed that the national government ultimately could use more force against local resistance.

The Little Rock school board approved a gradual desegregation plan that called for desegregating the city's Central High School first. Nine courageous African-American teenagers volunteered to desegregate the high school. Governor Faubus directed the state's National Guard to prevent desegregation, and, with a crowd cheering them on, the troops turned the nine students back when they tried to go to school on September 3, 1957.

The federal courts ordered Faubus to stop interfering with desegregation. When Faubus took the National Guard away from Central High, a near-riot broke out as the nine students again tried to attend. Now President Eisenhower got involved. After all, the state was directly defying an order from a federal court. If the Constitution meant anything, that couldn't stand. Eisenhower put the state's National Guard under federal control and ordered federal troops to protect the students at Central High. Each day for the next year the students went to school with military men around the school and in the halls.

The city school board tried to get out from under the desegregation order, pointing to the turmoil in the schools as a reason for further delay. When an appellate court agreed, the Supreme Court stepped in. Convening a special session, the Court met to hear the city's attorney argue against Thurgood Marshall and the United States government.

Again Frankfurter thought it possible to encourage the good white people of the South to take a stand against lawlessness, through an opinion

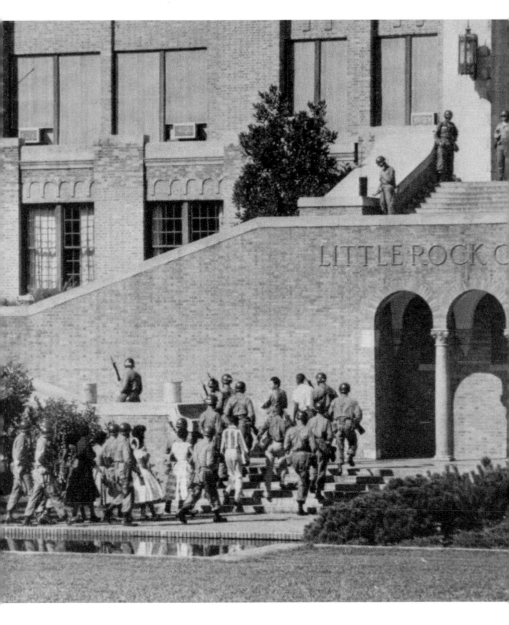

Federal troops protect black students integrating
Little Rock Central High School in 1957.

that rejected Faubus but praised the school board for trying as hard as it had to desegregate. Warren and the rest of the Court insisted on chastising violent resistance more severely than Frankfurter wanted.

Marshall captured what was at stake in his oral argument. The school board worried about disrupting education, but, Marshall said, "education is the teaching of the overall citizenship," and "I don't know of any more horrible destruction of [the] principle of citizenship than to tell young children that, those of you who withdrew, rather than go to school with Negroes . . . Come back, all is forgiven, you win." He said he knew who to worry about, the white children "who are told, as young people, that the way to get your rights is to violate the law and defy the lawful authorities. . . . I don't worry about those Negro kids' future. They've been struggling with democracy long enough. They know about it."

Marshall's appeal to the rule of law fit perfectly with the justices' concerns. The Court issued an opinion in an unusual form: Instead of saying either that it was "per curiam," meaning "by the court" as a whole, or that it was by a single justice joined by the others, the Court's opinion listed the names of all nine justices as its author, to emphasize each justice's personal commitment to *Brown*. The opinion, which actually had been written primarily by Justice William J. Brennan, a member of the Court since 1956, was forthright and stern. It acknowledged difficulties in desegregating Little Rock, but blamed those problems on Governor Faubus and the legislature's "determination to resist" *Brown*. The desegregation decision was "the supreme Law of the Land," and "[n]o state legislator or executive or judicial officer can act against the Constitution without violating his undertaking to support it." The principles *Brown* announced "and the obedience of the States to them . . . are indispensable to the protection of the freedoms guaranteed by our fundamental charter for all of us. Our constitutional ideal of equal justice under law is thus made a living truth."

Southern resistance to desegregation succeeded for a decade. By 1964 only about 1 percent of the Deep South's African-American children were attending schools with *any* white students. (Desegregation was more successful in border states like Delaware and Kentucky.)

The situation began to change when the 1964 Civil Rights Act directed the federal government to deny financial assistance to schools that discriminated on the basis of race. The Department of Health, Education, and Welfare (HEW) developed guidelines to identify districts where segregation persisted, using the ratio of white to African-American students in each school and the number of substantially one-race schools as measures. The threat of a funding cutoff was enough to induce many school districts to begin the desegregation process, although the sanction was so severe that Washington politicians were quite reluctant actually to use it.

Writing for a Supreme Court that had gotten fed up with the South's resistance, Justice Black ordered the federal courts to insist that the Prince Edward County schools reopen as desegregated schools. "There has been entirely too much deliberation and not enough speed," Black wrote. "The time for mere 'deliberate speed' has run out." The lower federal courts soon endorsed the HEW guidelines, and used them not simply to threaten a funding cutoff but to develop desegregation require-

Thurgood Marshall as Supreme Court justice

ments that the courts themselves would enforce. If a district had too many one-race schools, the federal courts would demand that the district eliminate them and try to make sure that the ratio of whites to African-American students in each school was roughly the same as the ratio throughout the district as a whole.

Complying with these requirements transformed the desegregation issue, finally resolving on the level of the law the question of whether the Constitution merely required desegregation or affirmatively required integration. According to the law as it developed, districts had to be integrated. But, in resolving the legal question, the courts opened up two far more difficult social and political questions.

The questions arose because, by the mid-1960s if not before, residential separation of the races had a large impact on racial attendance patterns. Sometimes residential separation resulted at least in part from government decisions. The federal mortgage insurance program, for example, had refused to insure homes bought by African-Americans in white neighborhoods in the years right after World War II, when a building boom established neighborhood patterns that persisted through the 1960s. When school boards built new schools in the middle of residential areas dominated by one race, rather on the border between areas, they contributed to continuing racial separation, because parents naturally wanted to live as close to their children's schools as they could. Sometimes, however, residential separation resulted from choices by prejudiced white home buyers, who simply didn't want to live near African-Americans, and by both whites and African-Americans who simply were more comfortable in neighborhoods where most of the people were like them in many ways, including race.

Residential segregation was widespread in the 1960s. As a result, so were one-race schools. To get each school to represent the district's overall racial proportions, children would have to go to schools outside their neighborhoods. Many parents didn't like that, and "busing" to achieve integration became a hot political issue as HEW prodded—and federal courts ordered—school districts to integrate their schools.

Once the federal courts focused on whether districts had too many one-race schools, they inevitably had to grapple with the question of whether what they called *de facto* segregation— racial separation that didn't result from government decisions separating the races—was just as unconstitutional as *de jure* segregation—segregation required by law. The strand in *Brown* that condemned separate schools as inherently unequal supported the judgment that *de facto* segregation *was* unconstitutional, while the strand that emphasized the importance of separation enforced by law supported the contrary judgment.

The Supreme Court has not, even by 1995, resolved that question. Instead, it discovered government decisions that produced segregation. Rather than holding that only statutes requiring that the races be separate amounted to *de jure* segregation, the Court extended the concept to include school location decisions intended to guarantee that few African-Americans would attend schools with whites, school board decisions drawing neighborhood school zones that fence African-Americans out of the zones including the district's whites, and the like.

The Court really had to extend its rules in that

direction. Otherwise recalcitrant school districts could get away with policies that were intended to, and did, reproduce the conditions that *Brown* had found unconstitutional. North Carolina's student assignment policies, for example, didn't expressly refer to race, but everyone knew that the point of adopting them was to ensure that almost no desegregation would occur.

The Court faced up to this problem in a 1968 case from eastern Virginia. New Kent County was a largely rural district, with enough students to support two high schools. Before *Brown,* of course, one school was used by whites and the other by African-Americans. After Virginia's massive resistance campaign collapsed, the New Kent County school board had a choice of what to do. It might have adopted a neighborhood school policy. If it had, the high schools would have been substantially integrated, because the rural district was not residentially segregated. Instead, the board adopted a "freedom of choice" plan, under which students were allowed to choose which school to attend. Not surprisingly, no whites chose to go to the former black school, and very few African-Americans were willing to subject themselves to the harassment they knew they would face in the formerly white school. So, under the freedom-of-choice plan, racial separation persisted.

The Court found the plan unconstitutional. And, after all, what could explain the board's decision to adopt the freedom-of-choice plan over the neighborhood school plan except a desire to perpetuate segregated conditions? If *Brown* meant anything, however, it had to mean that choosing a policy simply because the white majority didn't want their children to associate with African-Americans in school was unconstitutional.

The New Kent County decision further fueled the courts' move toward suspicion of *de facto* segregation. Politics did the same. African-Americans in Northern cities faced the same *de facto* separation that existed in the South, and they began to press the courts for relief. White Southerners began to resent what they regarded as different treatment; as they saw it, by the mid-1960s conditions in the South weren't that different from those in the North, and yet whites in the North didn't face the same pressures from HEW and the federal courts to deal with those conditions.

As the courts began to consider *de facto* segregation, a new issue arose. *De facto* segregation occurred because African-Americans and whites lived in different neighborhoods, often in widely separated parts of their districts. To eliminate *de facto* segregation, students would have to travel across the districts. Many white and African-American parents were troubled by busing students across town. Busing made it harder for parents to get to the schools to meet teachers or see their children in school events, and it made it harder for students to remain at school late for extracurricular activities. That made busing students to eliminate segregation controversial. Still, students in rural districts had been bused to school for many years, and sometimes it seemed that opposition to busing arose as much from a desire to retain *de facto* segregation as from real concern about the educational problems it could create.

The Republican party, which since the Eisenhower era had wanted to establish a political base in the South, saw the "busing" issue as the vehicle for its Southern strategy. With the election of Richard Nixon in 1968, the federal government's executive agencies began to pull back on their support of desegregation, both South and North. Nixon's four appointees to the Supreme Court— Chief Justice Warren Burger and Justices Harry Blackmun, Lewis Powell, and William Rehnquist— agreed that the federal courts had gone too far in attempting to alleviate conditions that, they believed, were caused mainly by the private choices of individuals and not by government policies.

The Supreme Court never repudiated the narrowest interpretation of *Brown,* and repeatedly upheld lower court decisions requiring school districts to remedy the continuing effects of their *own* prior decisions that caused segregated conditions. It also never held that *de facto* segregation alone was unconstitutional. In 1973 Justice Powell offered his colleagues a deal: find *de facto* segregation unconstitutional and extend the scope of the courts' control to urban districts throughout the North, but sharply limit busing as a remedy for segregation, whether *de facto* or *de jure*. Powell's liberal colleagues didn't accept the offer, and the Court continued to stumble around in its efforts to fit racial separation in the schools into its model of *de jure* segregation.

Earlier the Court had been unanimous in condemning segregation, and its members strove to speak with a single voice because they correctly believed that divisions on the Court would make it difficult to carry out the Court's orders. As the Court became divided over "busing" and *de facto* segregation, that is exactly what happened. Lower federal courts struggled on, trying to do what the now-divided Supreme Court said they should but finding it increasingly difficult to do so in the face of political opposition from the federal executive branch and legal qualms raised by members of the Supreme Court itself.

The Court itself wrote the final word on whether it would insist on integration, although it did so quite indirectly. The populations of the nation's cities became increasingly African-American and Hispanic, as whites moved from the cities to their suburbs. Achieving integration within a city school district became nearly impossible. (Some school districts, such as the one including Charlotte, North Carolina, actually were large enough to include most of the city's suburbs, but that was unusual.) To assure that African-American children in substantial numbers would attend the same schools as white children, suburban school districts had to participate in the integration effort.

Federal judges in Richmond, Virginia, and Detroit, Michigan, saw the logic of including suburban districts in their orders. They ordered desegregation plans that reached into the suburbs; in Detroit, for example, Judge Stephen Roth designed attendance zones shaped like pieces of a pie, extending from a narrow sliver in downtown Detroit to wider areas in the suburbs. In 1974 the Supreme Court said that Judge Roth shouldn't have done so. Unless the suburban districts themselves had adopted policies that contributed to racial separation, the federal courts couldn't include them in a remedy for unconstitutional actions taken by the city's officials.

Without the power to include suburban districts in desegregation plans, federal courts could do little to end the largely one-race composition of urban schools. So, although the Supreme Court's doctrines pointed in the direction of disapproving *de facto* segregation without quite saying so, its decision in the Detroit case meant that *de facto* segregation of the schools in the nation's cities would continue.

Today African-Americans are more likely to attend one-race schools in the urbanized Northeast and Midwest than they are in the more rural South: At the end of the 1980s 24 percent of African-American children in the South went to schools with 90 to 100 percent African-American enrollment, whereas 48 percent in the Northeast and 42 percent in the Midwest went to such schools. As one critic pointed out, African-American families moving from the South to a Northern city were *more* likely to find that their children would never attend a school with a white student than if they stayed in the South.

# Chapter 7
# THE VERDICT OF HISTORY

What, then, had *Brown* accomplished? If its direct effects on schools were small, its indirect effects were large. *Brown* contributed to the development of the modern civil rights movement. After World War II African-Americans throughout the country had stepped up their civil rights activities both in politics and on the streets. Their increased numbers in the North gave them more political power. The experience of fighting for democracy abroad to return to discrimination at home fueled their discontent. The struggle with the Soviet Union over which superpower stood for true democracy—a struggle sometimes fought to obtain influence in African nations that were on the verge of obtaining independence—strengthened their hand in dealing with national elites who found Southern segregation a particular embarrassment.

Although it would be easy to overestimate the

contribution *Brown* made to the modern civil rights movement, the Court's decision did add something to the movement's claims. Civil rights leaders repeatedly invoked *Brown* in their political and moral arguments against segregation. In planning a "freedom ride" on buses through the South, where an integrated group of passengers would attempt to desegregate the bus stations they stopped at, civil rights leaders scheduled the ride to end in New Orleans on May 17, 1961, *Brown*'s anniversary.

The most important civil rights demonstrations after *Brown* took place in Montgomery, Alabama, in 1955–56. The African-American community there had been troubled by what it regarded as the city's unfair *use* of the separate-but-equal rule on the city's buses. In December 1955, after an earlier challenge petered out, the community mobilized around the arrest of Rosa Parks, an NAACP activist who was arrested for refusing to move to the back of a bus when a white passenger got on. At first the protest, which took the form of a boycott of the city's bus system, aimed simply at making sure that bus operators treated African-American passengers respectfully. Within two months, however, the protest turned against segregation itself, in part because lawyers associated with the NAACP told the community's leaders that they would not provide legal assistance unless the leaders took on the separate-but-equal doctrine.

Long-standing community outrage at unfair treatment was the primary cause for the Montgomery bus boycott, but the protesters invoked *Brown* to justify their actions. Four days after *Brown* was decided, a community leader wrote the city's mayor threatening a boycott. The day the boycott started, Martin Luther King, Jr., who became a national civil rights leader as a result of his actions in Montgomery, referred to *Brown* in telling listeners in Montgomery, "If we are wrong, the Constitution of the United States is wrong."

*Brown* played a more direct role in the boycott's ultimate success. The city's white leadership tried to break the boycott. At first they tried enforcing traffic regulations against volunteers who offered to drive the city's African-Americans to work, to replace their usual bus trips. Eventually they settled on a legal strategy, and filed a suit in state court seeking an order barring anyone from operating a coordinated transportation system like the car pools. The case was to be heard by one of the state's most racist judges, Walter Jones. (In July 1956 Judge Jones started the process that led to the NAACP's shutdown in Alabama.) The judge surely would have entered the order, which would have meant that anyone involved in the boycott could be held in contempt of court.

Judge Jones never did enter such an order, though. After the boycott started, lawyers for the African-American community filed a federal lawsuit challenging the segregated bus system and asking specifically that *Plessy v. Ferguson,* which had involved transportation, be expressly overruled. The lower court handling the case felt that it couldn't reject *Plessy* no matter how strongly it felt that *Brown* undermined the 1896 decision; only the Supreme Court could overrule one of its own decisions. The lawyers appealed to the Supreme Court.

On the same day that the Alabama judge was about to enter his order, the Supreme Court reversed the lower court in the Montgomery case, explicitly overruled *Plessy,* and made it unnecessary to continue a boycott that might have been halted by the order everyone expected from the Alabama court. Someone in Judge Jones's courtroom that morning reportedly cried out, "God Almighty has spoken from Washington!"

Had the Montgomery bus boycott failed, the civil rights movement might have been stopped at an early stage. *Brown* provided the predicate for the Supreme Court's decision overruling *Plessy,* and in this indirect way allowed the civil rights movement to go forward.

*Brown*'s indirect effects went even deeper. Many people take the Constitution to express the nation's deepest moral commitments. When the Supreme Court said that segregation could not be reconciled with the Constitution, it told the nation that segregation was *wrong.* Civil rights leaders had been saying that for years, of course. Getting the Supreme Court, devoted to the rule of law and defining through constitutional law what the nation's highest aspirations were, to say so as well gave the moral argument against segregation much greater force.

The writings of Martin Luther King, Jr., are filled with references to the Constitution. Race discrimination "rendered [the Constitution] inoperative in vast areas of the nation," King wrote. The civil rights movement, he believed, would advance the "goals" of the Constitution. The Constitution in the United States has sometimes been called our civil religion. Had the Supreme Court refused to repudiate the separate-but-equal doctrine—even if it had tried to force the South to take the "equal" part of the doctrine seriously—King would have been unable to bolster his religious and moral case against segregation with his appeal to the nation's civil religion.

Getting the rest of the nation to act on the judgment that segregation was wrong was another matter. Political leaders had to be persuaded that they would be better off if they joined the crusade against discrimination. That took many more years, as African-Americans protested in the streets, through "sit-ins" at segregated lunch counters, and with marches protesting voting discrimination. The moral energy for these activities came from religion, a sense of justice, and much more. But, at least in part, it also came from the conviction that, as the Supreme Court had said in *Brown,* race discrimination was not only wrong, it was unconstitutional.

What had happened in the districts involved in *Brown*? By 1994 the Washington, D.C., schools were almost entirely one-race; only about 4 percent of the students attending the schools were white, and those were concentrated in a handful of schools in the richer area of the city. Washington was ringed by suburbs in Maryland and Virginia, to which many whites and African-Americans moved as the city became less safe, and those suburbs were continuing to struggle with problems of *de facto* segregation.

In 1979 Linda Brown signed on to a lawsuit reviving the original case against Topeka. There too residential segregation meant that schools on the city's East Side had more than their share of the city's African-American children and those on the West Side more white children. The state froze school district boundaries, which meant that suburban school districts couldn't be brought into a desegregation plan. The city had tried to overcome *de facto* segregation by closing some schools, redrawing attendance zones, and allowing voluntary transfers between schools when that would bring both schools closer to the city's overall ratio of African-Americans to whites. The federal court hearing Linda Brown's case found that the city hadn't done enough to overcome the heritage of segregation. It proposed to close several school on the East Side and build two "magnet" schools to attract white children to programs emphasizing environmental and computer science. "Magnet" schools were widely thought to be an attractive alternative to more extensive mandatory student assignment policies, which would require many children to ride buses to their assigned schools. The record on magnet schools has been mixed. Some do end up substantially integrated, while others have failed to attract enough white students to produce integrated classes. Again the federal court rejected the plan and asked the city to come up with a better plan. The case remained unresolved in mid-1995.

Districts could have overcome the hurdles caused by residential segregation if they had been able to draw their suburbs into desegregation plans. Some cities tried to operate voluntary programs, getting suburban districts to agree to take in students from the central city. The Supreme Court's 1974 decision involving Detroit said that the federal courts couldn't *order* a remedy that combined city and suburban school districts, except under special and rare conditions. That shut off the only effective route to substantial integration of the public schools in our largest cities.

The Wilmington schools were integrated, but only because the federal courts found that the special conditions for including suburban districts in a desegregation plan were satisfied.

In Summerton, Harry Briggs lost his job and the family had to leave town. None of the Briggs children went to college. In 1994 there was only a single white child in the county's high school, and only about fourteen in the elementary schools. All the other white children attended a private Christian academy, founded by parents who refused to accept desegregation of any sort. Summerton's high school ranked among the state's lowest in academic achievement. The town council was all-white.

Barbara Johns's family sent her to finish high school in Alabama, and she eventually moved to Philadelphia. Prince Edward County's schools were closed from 1959 to 1964. After reopening they struggled to draw white students back from the private—and segregated—academies they had gone to while the schools were closed. The Farmville city council had a five-person majority that strongly supported the all-white academy, with three dissenters regularly losing votes to increase spending on the public schools. African-Americans filed a suit in 1993 charging that Farmville's voting system froze African-Americans out of political power.

By 1994 Prince Edward County's schools were 27 percent white (in a district where whites were 62 percent of the adult population). Guided by a superintendent who emphasized traditional quality education, and despite the financial constraints the schools faced, they were regarded as probably the best in Virginia's southern counties.

The impact of desegregation in the districts involved in *Brown v. Board of Education* was more ambiguous than desegregation's supporters had hoped when they began the lawsuits in Topeka, Prince Edward County, and Clarendon County. Perhaps *Brown* was only a partial success in terms of improving the quality of education for African-Americans and whites. Still, the Supreme Court's pronouncements that the principle of segregation was unacceptable in our constitutional system gave heart to those who sought to eliminate all forms of racial segregation. Even today *Brown* stands as the Court's deepest statement on the central issue in American history—how Americans of all races should treat one another. In that sense it is a triumph for American constitutionalism.

# FOR FURTHER READING

The classic treatment of *Brown v. Board of Education* itself is Richard Kluger, *Simple Justice* (New York: Knopf, 1975). A broader overview, focusing on Thurgood Marshall and carrying the story through 1961, is Mark Tushnet, *Making Civil Rights Law: Thurgood Marshall and the Supreme Court, 1935–1961* (New York: Oxford University Press, 1994). Even broader, examining the entire history of the Supreme Court's constitutional decisions on race-related issues, is Loren Miller, *The Petitioners* (New York: Pantheon Books, 1966). Taylor Branch, *Parting the Waters: America in the King Years, 1954–1963* (New York: Simon & Schuster, 1988), is a prizewinning survey of race relations during the period. A good study of massive resistance is Numan Bartley, *The Rise of Massive Resistance: Race and Politics in the South During the 1950s* (Baton Rouge: Lousiana State University Press, 1969); Robbins Gates, *The*

*Making of Massive Resistance: Virginia's Politics of School Desegregation, 1954–1956* (Chapel Hill: University of North Carolina Press, 1962), focuses on a single state. Bob Smith, *They Closed Their Schools: Prince Edward County, Virginia, 1951–1964* (Chapel Hill: University of North Carolina Press, 1965), describes the effects of massive resistance in Prince Edward County.

# INDEX

**139**

# ABOUT THE
# AUTHOR

Mark V. Tushnet, associate dean and professor of
law at Georgetown University Law Center, was the
law clerk for Supreme Court justice Thurgood
Marshall, the distinguished former Civil Rights
attorney who had argued *Brown v. Board of
Education* before the Supreme Court. Tushnet is
the author of the adult book *Making Civil Rights
Law: Thurgood Marshall and the Supreme Court,
1935–1961*.